3327

Climate and the Environment

WORLD ALMANAC® LIBRARY

Please visit our web site at: www.worldalmanaclibrary.com
For a free color catalog describing World Almanac® Library's list
of high-quality books and multimedia programs, call 1-800-848-2928
or fax your request to (414) 332-3567.

The editors at World Almanac® Library would like to thank Dr. Jonathan D. Kahl, Professor of Atmospheric Sciences, University of Wisconsin-Milwaukee, for the technical expertise and advice he brought to the production of this book.

Library of Congress Cataloging-in-Publication Data

Climate and the environment.
      p. cm. — (21st century science)
    Summary: Describes Earth's environment and various climates, as well as the damage being done by air, water, and soil pollution to the Earth and its inhabitants.
    Includes bibliographical references and index.
    ISBN 0-8368-5006-8 (lib. bdg.)
    1. Climatology—Juvenile literature. 2. Environmental sciences—Juvenile literature. [1. Climatology.
2. Environmental sciences. 3. Pollution.] I. Title. II. Series.
QC981.3.C58 2002
551.6—dc21   2002022705

This North American edition first published in 2002 by
World Almanac® Library
330 West Olive Street, Suite 100
Milwaukee, WI 53212 USA

Created and produced as the *Visual Guide to Understanding Climate and the Environment* by
QA INTERNATIONAL
329 rue de la Commune Ouest, 3ᵉ étage
Montreal, Québec
Canada H2Y 2E1
Tel: (514) 499-3000 Fax: (514) 499-3010
www.qa-international.com

© QA International, 2001

Publisher: Jacques Fortin

Editorial Director: François Fortin

Executive Editor: Serge D'Amico

Illustrations Editor: Marc Lalumière

Art Director: Rielle Lévesque

Graphic Designer: Anne Tremblay

Writers: Stéphane Batigne, Josée Bourbonnière, Nathalie Fredette, Agence Science-Presse

Computer Graphic Artists: Jean-Yves Ahern, Maxime Bigras, Patrice Blais, Yan Bohler, Mélanie Boivin, Charles Campeau, Jocelyn Gardner, Jonathan Jacques, Alain Lemire, Raymond Martin, Nicolas Oroc, Carl Pelletier, Simon Pelletier, Frédérick Simard, Mamadou Togola, Yan Tremblay

Researchers: Anne-Marie Brault, Jessie Daigle, Anne-Marie Villeneuve, Kathleen Wynd

Translation: Käthe Roth

Copy Editor: Jane Broderick

Production: Mac Thien Nguyen Hoang

Prepress: Tony O'Riley

Page Layout: Véronique Boisvert, Lucie Mc Brearty, Geneviève Théroux Béliveau

Reviewers: Gilles Brien, Yves Comeau, Frédéric Fabry, David B. Frost, Mario Laquerre, Marc Olivier, Judith Patterson

World Almanac® Library Editor: Alan Wachtel

World Almanac® Library Art Direction: Tammy Gruenewald

Cover Design: Katherine A. Goedheer

Photo credits: abbreviations: t = top, c = center, b = bottom, r = right, l = left
p. 13 (cr) (Baobab): Papilio/CORBIS/Magma; p. 17 (r) (Vineyards): Charles O'Rear/CORBIS/Magma; p. 17 (tr) (Coniferous forest): Raymond Gehman/CORBIS/Magma; p. 45 (c) (Smog): Dean Conger/CORBIS/Magma; p. 46 (t) (Corrosion): Ecoscene/CORBIS/Magma; p. 51 (bl) (Oil spill): Ecoscene/CORBIS/Magma.

Printed in Canada

1 2 3 4 5 6 7 8 9 06 05 04 03 02

Table of Contents

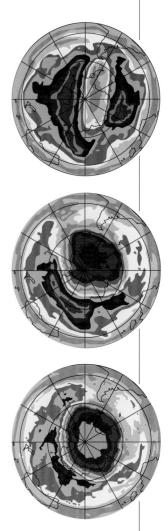

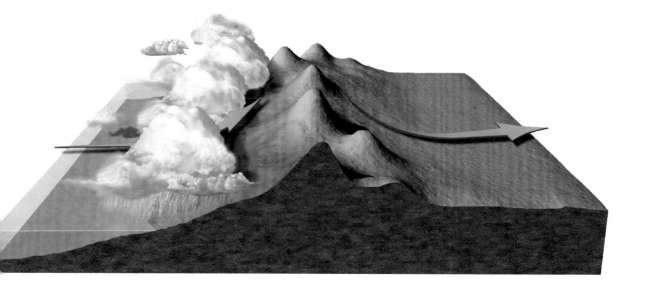

While cold, dry winds sculpt the sand dunes of Saudi Arabia's Nefud Desert, monsoon rains saturate the coastal lands of India. The ground of northern Siberia, in Russia, is frozen for much of the year, while the British Isles enjoy much milder temperatures. Earth's varied mosaic of climates is due to a complex combination of many meteorological, geological, and geographical factors.

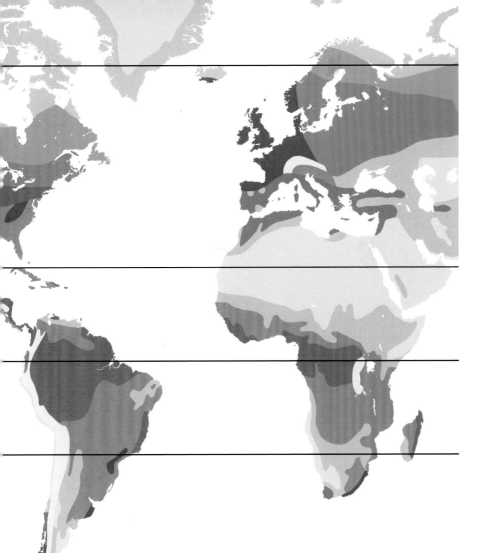

Earth's Climates

The Seasonal Cycle

The effect of Earth's inclination

Contrary to popular belief, the cycle of the seasons—that is, the periodic change of climate over the months of the year—is due not to Earth's distance from the Sun, but to its inclination. Our planet's axis of rotation leans at an angle of about 23.5° in relation to the ecliptic, or the path of Earth's orbit. This inclination is directly responsible for the variation in sunshine hours, and, thus, the succession of seasons, throughout the year. The same feature explains why the seasons take place at opposite times of year in Earth's two hemispheres; summer in the Southern Hemisphere always coincides with winter in the Northern Hemisphere.

The **summer solstice**—June 21 or 22 in the Northern Hemisphere—is the longest day of the year and the first day of the summer season. In summer, the Sun rises high in the sky and heats the atmosphere.

SUMMER SOLSTICE

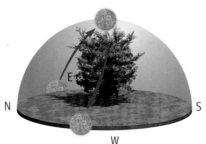

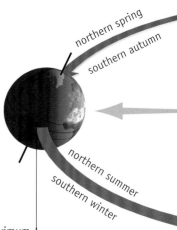

northern spring
southern autumn
northern summer
southern winter

Earth is at its **aphelion**, or maximum distance from the Sun, on July 3, when the two are 94.5 million miles (152.1 million kilometers) apart. The heat in the Northern Hemisphere on this date is due to Earth's inclination.

On June 21, **summer** begins in Algiers, Algeria, located in the Northern Hemisphere.

On June 21, **winter** begins in Cape Town, South Africa, in the Southern Hemisphere.

THE ANGLE OF INCIDENCE OF THE SUN'S RAYS

The temperature on Earth's surface is directly related to the angle at which the Sun's rays penetrate the atmosphere. Where this angle of incidence is low, making the rays skim the ground, solar energy is dispersed. In contrast, it is hottest where the rays hit the ground at a 90° angle.

Because of Earth's inclination, solar rays reach the Northern Hemisphere at a high angle during the months of June, July, and August, causing the summer season. At the same time, rays hit the Southern Hemisphere at a low angle, making it winter there.

SPRING EQUINOX

The **vernal equinox** occurs on March 20 or 21 in the Northern Hemisphere. On this day, spring begins, the Sun rises directly in the east and sets directly in the west, and day and night are of equal lengths.

On January 3, Earth is at its closest position to the Sun, or **perihelion**, only 91.5 million miles (147.3 million km) away from it.

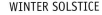

northern winter

southern summer

Sun

northern autumn

southern spring

WINTER SOLSTICE

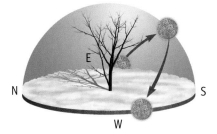

The shortest day of the year in the Northern Hemisphere, called the **winter solstice,** is December 21 or 22. On this day, as winter begins, the Sun stays low, heating the atmosphere only slightly.

AUTUMNAL EQUINOX

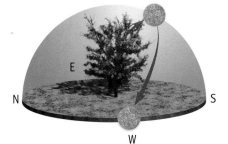

On September 22 or 23, day and night are of equal duration. In the Northern Hemisphere, this is the first day of fall, or the **autumnal equinox**. As with the vernal equinox, the Sun rises directly in the east and sets directly in the west.

THE INFLUENCE OF LATITUDE ON AMOUNT OF DAYLIGHT					
	Poles	**Helsinki (60°)**	**Montreal (45°)**	**Cairo (30°)**	**Equator**
summer solstice	24 hours	19 hours	16 hours	14 hours	12 hours
vernal equinox	12 hours	12 hours	12 hours	12 hours	12 hours
winter solstice	0 hours	6 hours	8 hours	10 hours	12 hours
autumnal equinox	12 hours	12 hours	12 hours	12 hours	12 hours

Climates of the World

From one extreme to another

Earth's various regions have very different climates in terms of temperature, precipitation, humidity, and wind. The distribution of climatic zones on the surface of the planet is dictated mainly by latitude. Conditions related to the amount of sunlight received in an area, such as length of day, change of seasons, and angle of solar rays, in fact, play the largest role in determining climate. But many other factors, including land use, dominant winds, altitude, relief features, and ocean currents, also enter the picture.

CLIMATOGRAMS

Climatograms are used to compare climates in different places. These charts show average temperatures (upper black lines) and average precipitation levels (bars) for each month of the year.

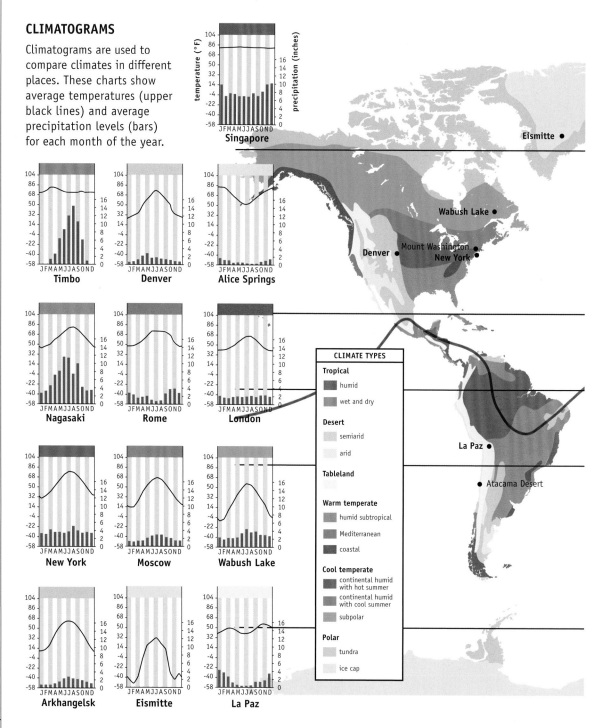

CLIMATE TYPES

Tropical
- humid
- wet and dry

Desert
- semiarid
- arid

Tableland

Warm temperate
- humid subtropical
- Mediterranean
- coastal

Cool temperate
- continental humid with hot summer
- continental humid with cool summer
- subpolar

Polar
- tundra
- ice cap

SOME RECORDS			
maximum temperature	136°F (57.8°C)	El Azizia, Libya	September 13, 1922
minimum temperature	−128.6°F (−89.2°C)	Vostok, Antarctica	July 21, 1983
maximum annual precipitation	1,043 in (26,461 mm)	Cherrapunji, India	1860–1861
minimum annual precipitation	0 in (0 mm)	Atacama Desert, Chile	1903–1918
highest air pressure	1,083.8 hPa	Agata, Russia	December 31, 1968
lowest air pressure	870 hPa	Typhoon Tip (Pacific Ocean)	October 12, 1979
strongest wind	230 mph (371 km/h)	Mount Washington, United States	April 12, 1934

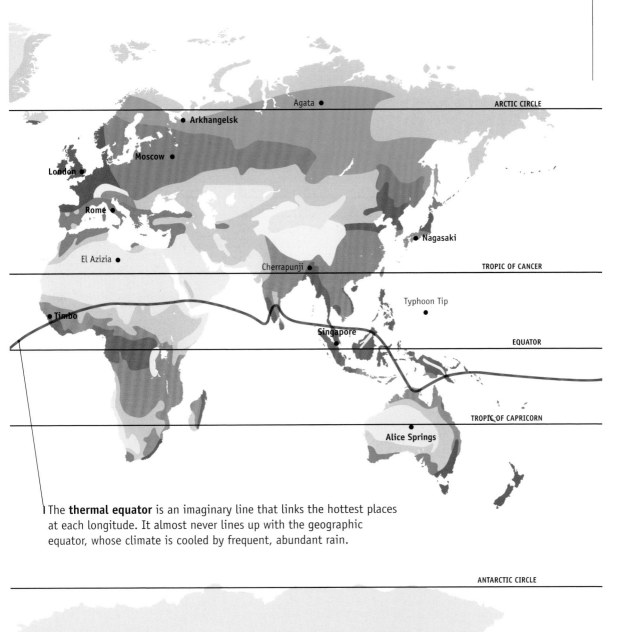

The **thermal equator** is an imaginary line that links the hottest places at each longitude. It almost never lines up with the geographic equator, whose climate is cooled by frequent, abundant rain.

Desert Climates

Always the dry season

One quarter of the planet's landmass—about 13.5 million square miles (35 million square kilometers)—has an arid or semiarid climate. These regions, including the Sahara Desert, the Gobi Desert, and the Mongolian Steppes, all have very low levels of precipitation. Their vegetation, because it rarely and irregularly receives rainfall, develops slowly, and the ground is almost entirely bare. In most cases, this dryness is related to the presence of semipermanent anticyclones, but other geographic factors may also be at work.

DESERTS WITH HIGH ATMOSPHERIC PRESSURE

Air heated by solar rays over the equator rises through convection ❶. As it rises, the air cools and discharges its humidity as heavy rain ❷. Then, when it reaches an altitude of 9 to 12 miles (15 to 20 km), the cool air moves toward the poles ❸. Now denser and, therefore, heavier, it descends ❹ toward the surface of Earth's tropical regions, located between 15° and 30° latitude. During its descent, the air is heated again and expands. This process maintains a high-pressure zone along the two subtropical belts ❺ located around 25° to 35° latitude. The Sahara, Nefud, Kalahari, and Great Sandy deserts are the main high-pressure deserts.

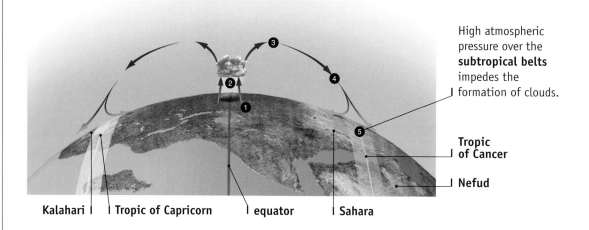

High atmospheric pressure over the **subtropical belts** impedes the formation of clouds.

⌐ Tropic of Cancer

⌐ Nefud

Kalahari | Tropic of Capricorn | equator | Sahara

THE INFLUENCE OF RELIEF FEATURES

Some arid regions owe their dryness to the configuration of the relief around them. When a mountain chain borders a coastal area, it removes much of the humidity contained in the oceanic air masses by orographic precipitation, or precipitation caused by the landscape. Regions in the lee of a mountainous barrier, therefore, receive very little rain. This is the case in the Patagonia, Great Basin, and Gobi deserts.

Crescent-shaped **dunes** can form with little sand but require the constant action of wind. The distance between their points varies between 100 and 1,000 feet (30 and 300 m). ⌐

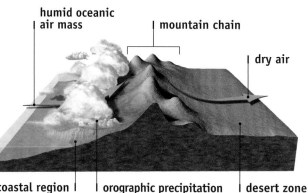

humid oceanic air mass | mountain chain

dry air

coastal region | orographic precipitation | desert zone

When **wind** pushes the sand, it ⌐ leaves long rocky stretches.

DISTRIBUTION OF DESERTS AND STEPPES

All continents have arid zones, called deserts, or semi-arid zones, also known as steppes. In regions around the tropics of Cancer and Capricorn, the climate is strongly related to the dryness of the air. The near-complete absence of cloud cover lets 90 percent of the solar rays through, causing a lack of water in the ground.

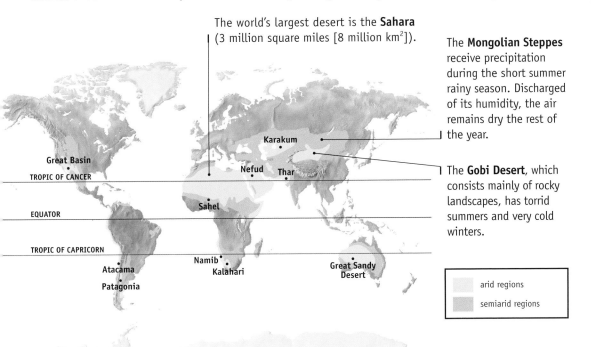

The world's largest desert is the **Sahara** (3 million square miles [8 million km²]).

The **Mongolian Steppes** receive precipitation during the short summer rainy season. Discharged of its humidity, the air remains dry the rest of the year.

The **Gobi Desert**, which consists mainly of rocky landscapes, has torrid summers and very cold winters.

Great Basin
TROPIC OF CANCER
Nefud
Thar
Karakum
Sahel
EQUATOR
TROPIC OF CAPRICORN
Atacama
Namib
Kalahari
Patagonia
Great Sandy Desert

- arid regions
- semiarid regions

WATER AND THE DESERT

In deserts, precipitation often occurs in the form of heavy showers that suddenly drop large amounts of water onto the dry, almost barren ground. Plateaus are carved out and faceted by flash floods in the wadis, which deposit sediment at the feet of cliffs and then dry very rapidly through evaporation and infiltration. The dryness of the air is responsible for the wide temperature swings that characterize deserts. The ground is very hot during the day and can freeze during the night, which causes rocks to break into pieces and accumulate in taluses at the feet of buttes.

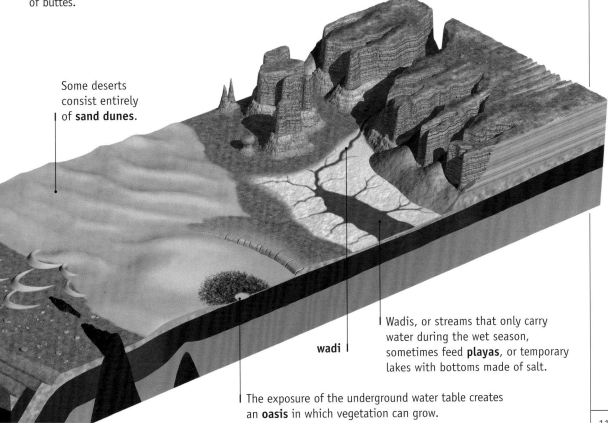

Some deserts consist entirely of **sand dunes**.

wadi

Wadis, or streams that only carry water during the wet season, sometimes feed **playas**, or temporary lakes with bottoms made of salt.

The exposure of the underground water table creates an **oasis** in which vegetation can grow.

Tropical Climates

Combinations of heat and humidity

Regions located on either side of the equator are subjected to high temperatures due to regular sunshine all year round. In these regions, there are two climatic zones, differentiated by their annual distribution of precipitation. The humid tropical climate features the high and constant humidity that favors the development of the equatorial forest. The wet and dry tropical climate, on the other hand, has a wet season with monsoon rains followed by a dry winter.

THE EQUATORIAL FOREST

There are no seasons in the humid tropical climatic zone. The high heat that prevails over equatorial regions throughout the year ensures a permanent zone of low atmospheric pressure with much cloud cover and regular precipitation.

These conditions enable life to flourish in the equatorial forest, which contains half of all living species on Earth, including 20 times more different species of trees than are found in temperate forests. Conditions differ greatly from the bottom to the top of the forest. At the top, the vegetation cover, or canopy, absorbs most solar radiation, while the shady understory is sheltered from light and wind.

In equatorial regions, day and night are of equal length all year round, guaranteeing stable levels of **sunlight** throughout the year.

Emerging trees, which grow to a height of almost 200 feet (60 m), serve as supports for long lianas and various other epiphytes, or plants that grow on other plants.

At a height of 100 to 150 feet (30 to 45 m), the **canopy** is the top level of the forest. Most tropical plant and animal species live here.

The **understory** of the tropical forest receives 100 times less sunlight than the top of the canopy. It is always shaded, and very little vegetation is able to grow there.

Decomposed plant matter is very quickly reused by other plants, which prevents the **soil** from becoming thick and rich.

Because trees in these forests cannot grow very deep roots, they are often propped up by **root buttresses**.

DISTRIBUTION OF TROPICAL CLIMATES

Both the Amazon and Congo river basins, located around the equator, and the littoral areas of Southeast Asia, northern Australia, and Central America have humid tropical climates. The wet and dry type of tropical climate is found mainly in Africa, South America, and Asia. Various types of vegetation, including dry tropical forest and savanna, develop in these regions, marking a transitional area between equatorial, semi-arid, and temperate zones.

With more than 430 inches (1,090 centimeters) of precipitation annually, **Cherrapunji, India** is the rainiest city in the world.

Equatorial forest covers 60 percent of the **Indonesian archipelago**.

Baobabs, the emblematic trees of the **African savanna**, store water in their trunks during the dry season.

TROPIC OF CANCER

EQUATOR

TROPIC OF CAPRICORN

| Congo basin

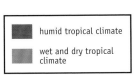

humid tropical climate

wet and dry tropical climate

Running through Brazil, Peru, Colombia, and Bolivia, the **Amazonian forest** has an area of more than 1.3 million square miles (3.5 million km²). It comprises 30 percent of all equatorial forestland in the world.

THE MONSOON CYCLE

The monsoon phenomenon is related to the seasonal movement of the intertropical convergence zone (ITCZ). The position of this low pressure zone, on which the trade winds of both hemispheres converge, changes throughout the year, influencing the climate in the intertropical regions. In January ❶, the ITCZ is located south of the equator. Winds bring precipitation to Indonesia and northern Australia. In July ❷, the ITCZ moves north, and the coasts of Southeast Asia and India receive monsoon rains.

| Indonesia

The **intertropical convergence zone** is the belt of low pressure that goes around Earth near the equator.

| India

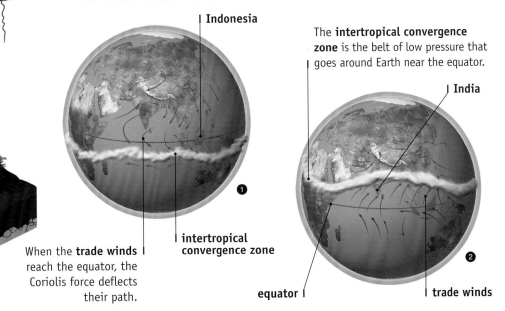

When the **trade winds** reach the equator, the Coriolis force deflects their path.

| intertropical convergence zone

❶

equator |

❷

| trade winds

Polar Climates

The kingdoms of cold

In the highest latitudes, the climate is dominated by polar air masses, which do not heat up much even during the long period of summer sunshine they receive. In the centers of Antarctica and Greenland, where temperatures never rise above 32°F (0°C), the ground remains permanently frozen and covered with a thick ice cap. The northern edges of Eurasia and North America have a more temperate climate, with summer temperatures rising above the freezing point. This rise in temperature enables a thin top layer of ground to thaw, which, in turn, allows tundra vegetation to grow.

SUNSHINE HOURS IN THE POLAR REGIONS

The amount of sunshine a region receives depends on its latitude. The nearer to the poles a place is located, the longer the days are in summer and the shorter they are in winter.

In Helsinki, Finland (60°N latitude), daylight lasts only six hours at the winter solstice but is 19 hours long at the summer solstice. The Repulse Bay base in Canada is located on the Arctic Circle (66°34' N latitude), an imaginary line that marks the edge of the region that experiences the "Midnight Sun." In this area, the Sun remains visible for several days in a row during midsummer. At Earth's northern and southern poles, there is daylight for six months and night for six months.

Although there are long periods of summer sunshine in the polar regions, the Sun never rises very high in the sky, and its rays hit the atmosphere at too low an angle to heat it much. In midsummer, the temperature in the middle of the Arctic Ocean, at the North Pole, barely rises above 32°F (0°C).

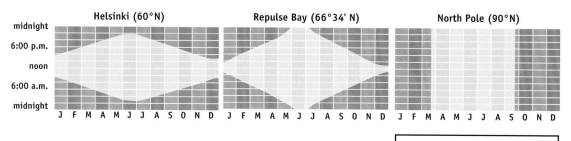

Helsinki (60°N) Repulse Bay (66°34' N) North Pole (90°N)

midnight
6:00 p.m.
noon
6:00 a.m.
midnight

J F M A M J J A S O N D   J F M A M J J A S O N D   J F M A M J J A S O N D

day   night

PACK ICE

In the coldest oceans on the planet, the water is covered by a permanent or seasonal layer of ice, called pack ice, whose thickness may reach 10 to 13 feet (3 to 4 m). In winter, Arctic pack ice ❶ covers over 4.5 million square miles (12 million km²), invading many fjords, bays, estuaries, and straits. Hudson Bay, which extends south to 51° latitude, is totally covered with ice.

Antarctica ❷, covered by an icecap, is also surrounded by pack ice. This pack ice shrinks in the summer but forms a huge sheet covering over 7.5 million square miles (20 million km²) in winter.

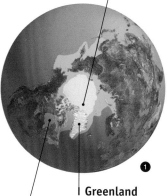

North Pole

Greenland

Hudson Bay

❶

ice cap

permanent pack ice

winter pack ice

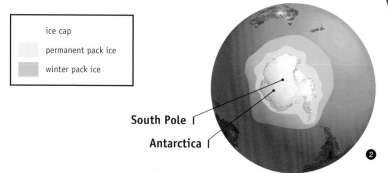

South Pole

Antarctica

❷

PERMAFROST

In the zones of North America and Asia that lie beyond the areas of permanent ice and snow, the lower layers of the ground beneath the soil, called permafrost, never thaw. Only a few patches of unfrozen land in these regions provide deep water circulation, connecting the water table to the surface. As the temperature rises in the spring, the top layer of the ground—called the mollisol, or active layer—thaws. The thickness of this layer varies from a few inches (cm) to a few yards (m), depending on latitude and temperature. If the mollisol is thin, tundra vegetation, which includes moss, lichens, grass, and dwarf shrubs, grows in it, while if it is thicker, taiga vegetation, such as coniferous trees and shrubs, grows in it.

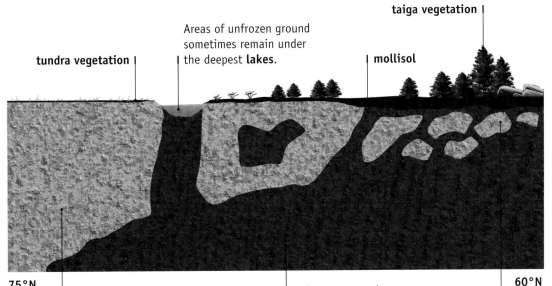

taiga vegetation

Areas of unfrozen ground sometimes remain under the deepest **lakes**.

tundra vegetation

mollisol

75°N

60°N

In the coldest regions, the **permafrost** is permanent and can reach over 1,300 feet (400 m) in depth.

unfrozen ground

discontinuous permafrost

low vegetation

marsh

THE TUNDRA IN SUMMER

When higher temperatures melt the snow cover, the ground absorbs the solar rays and its surface thaws. Water, blocked by the permafrost, cannot filter down, so it soaks the mollisol, forming marshes that are quickly covered with low, colorful vegetation.

Eroded rocks are a reminder that an ice cap covered the northern parts of the continents more than 10,000 years ago.

permafrost

mollisol

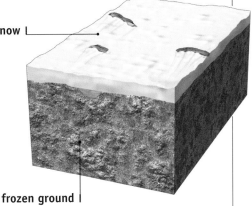

snow

THE TUNDRA IN WINTER

During the coldest months, the temperature may drop to –58°F (–50°C) in the tundra regions. The ground is totally frozen and covered with a thin layer of snow. In fact, the anticyclonic conditions above the tundra in winter make the air too dry for much precipitation to develop. Icy winds sweep the landscape, sometimes uncovering rocks.

frozen ground

Temperate Climates

Four distinct seasons

In the middle latitudes, there is great variation in the amount of sunlight per day over the course of the year, but sunshine never reaches the extreme durations that it does in the tropics and at the poles. The climate of the mid-latitude regions is called a temperate climate, having relatively gentle conditions and a cycle of four distinct seasons. Temperate climates are very diverse, since they are also influenced by geographic factors, such as continentality, altitude, and relief.

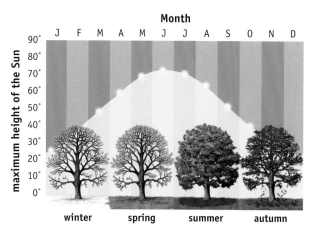

Month

J F M A M J J A S O N D

maximum height of the Sun

winter   spring   summer   autumn

AMOUNT OF SUNLIGHT AND SEASONS

Only regions located in the mid-latitudes have four distinct seasons. This cycle is directly related to variations in the number of daylight hours throughout the year. At 39° latitude, for example, the Sun's maximum height in the sky varies from 27.5° in winter to 74° in summer. The variation in the amount of sunlight per day influences the seasonal air temperatures. The effect of this variation is evident in the annual cycle of plants adapted to temperate climates.

At the alpine level, temperatures are too low—an annual average of only 36°F to 37°F (2°C to 3°C)—for trees to develop. Instead, **herbaceous vegetation,** or leafy, non-woody plants, grow.

The subalpine level, with its wide range of temperatures, is home to **conifers**.

Human activities are concentrated on the **valley floor,** where the climate is mild.

The **nival level** is extremely cold and the snow never melts. Except for a few types of lichens, there is no vegetation.

The humid, cool **mountain level** is favorable to mixed forests.

With an average annual temperature of 59°F (15°C), the climate of the **hill level** is very similar to that of the plains.

alpine level

subalpine level

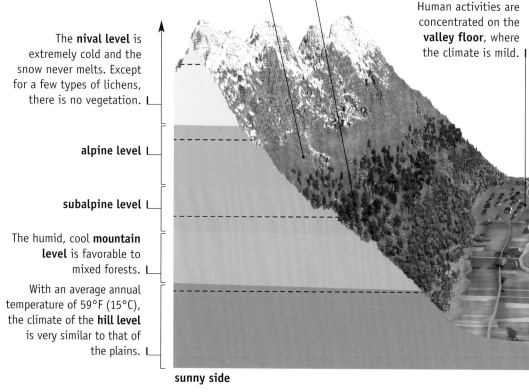

sunny side

THE OCEAN'S INFLUENCE

The Gulf Stream ❶ is one of the most powerful oceanic currents on the planet. After flowing north along the coast of North America to Newfoundland, its warm waters give rise to the North Atlantic Drift ❷. This warm current crosses the North Atlantic, heating the cold arctic air masses ❸ that it meets. It is largely responsible for the difference in climate between North America ❹, influenced by polar air, and western Europe ❺, where the warm, humid weather is typical of a coastal climate.

The coniferous forest is adapted to the subpolar climate found at 50° N latitude in **North America**.

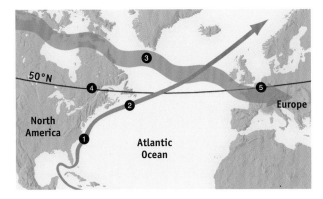

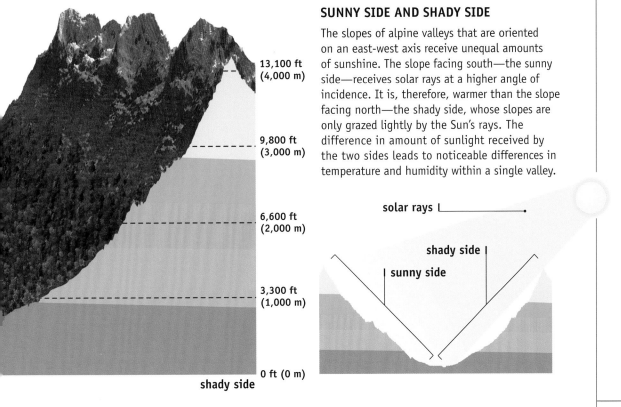

The warm air that blows over **Europe** makes it possible for grapevines to grow as far north as 50° N latitude.

MOUNTAIN CLIMATES

Because temperature drops as altitude rises, the slopes of a valley offer a succession of climates comparable to those one would find as one goes toward the poles. In the Alps, for example, the valley floors have climatic conditions similar to those in neighboring plains. Higher on the slopes, forests replace fields, and conifers become predominant, as in regions with a subpolar climate. At the alpine level, the climate resembles that of the arctic tundra, and trees give way to alpine pastures. Finally, the highest ground, permanently covered with snow, has the same kind of climate as the icecaps.

13,100 ft (4,000 m)

9,800 ft (3,000 m)

6,600 ft (2,000 m)

3,300 ft (1,000 m)

0 ft (0 m)

shady side

SUNNY SIDE AND SHADY SIDE

The slopes of alpine valleys that are oriented on an east-west axis receive unequal amounts of sunshine. The slope facing south—the sunny side—receives solar rays at a higher angle of incidence. It is, therefore, warmer than the slope facing north—the shady side, whose slopes are only grazed lightly by the Sun's rays. The difference in amount of sunlight received by the two sides leads to noticeable differences in temperature and humidity within a single valley.

solar rays

shady side

sunny side

El Niño and La Niña

How a current reversal causes climatic upheavals

The surface waters of the Pacific Ocean are normally pushed westward by the dominant winds called the trade winds. This large-scale phenomenon is responsible to a great extent for the climatic conditions that prevail over the entire Pacific region, and even beyond. The weakening and reversal of this westward push, known as El Niño, heats the eastern part of the ocean and causes major climatic upheavals. After one or two years of these upheavals, El Niño gives way to the opposite phenomenon, called La Niña, and then the situation returns to normal.

NORMAL OCEANIC AND ATMOSPHERIC CIRCULATION IN THE PACIFIC

The equatorial zone of the Pacific Ocean is normally affected by the trade winds ❶. Pushed by these constant winds, the surface water ❷ slowly moves from South America toward Southeast Asia, creating a buildup of warm water between the two continents. Evaporation ❸ of warm surface water causes clouds to form ❹, and the trade winds push these clouds westward. Warm, humid air ❺ rises near Asia, while masses of cool, dry air ❻ descend near the South American coast. This pattern of atmospheric circulation, called the Walker cell, affects the climate of the entire Pacific zone; while the seasonal monsoon rains ❼ pour down on Asia, an anticyclone ❽ settles in over the South American coast.

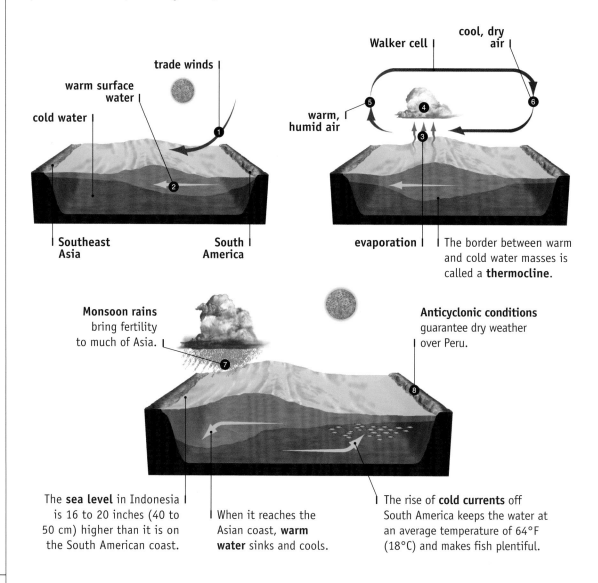

trade winds

warm surface water

cold water

Walker cell

cool, dry air

warm, humid air

| Southeast Asia | South America |

evaporation

The border between warm and cold water masses is called a **thermocline**.

Monsoon rains bring fertility to much of Asia.

Anticyclonic conditions guarantee dry weather over Peru.

The **sea level** in Indonesia is 16 to 20 inches (40 to 50 cm) higher than it is on the South American coast.

When it reaches the Asian coast, **warm water** sinks and cools.

The rise of **cold currents** off South America keeps the water at an average temperature of 64°F (18°C) and makes fish plentiful.

EL NIÑO: A REVERSAL OF OCEANIC AND ATMOSPHERIC CIRCULATION

For reasons that are still not clear, the trade winds are weaker in certain years. Pushed by strong west winds ❶, warm surface water ❷ spreads through the central and eastern parts of the Pacific Ocean, where it evaporates ❸. The Walker cell ❹ and the convective cells ❺ distributed around the globe at the equator are disturbed. A low pressure system (cyclone) ❻ is maintained in the eastern Pacific, while Southeast Asia is under a powerful high pressure system (anticyclone) ❼ that deprives it of the usual monsoon rains.

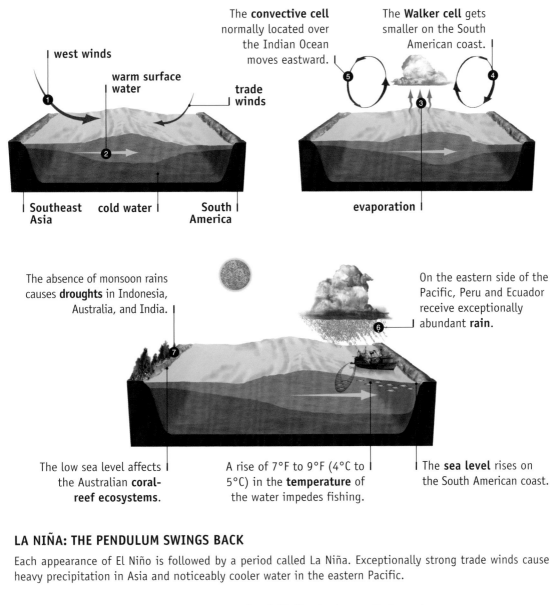

The **convective cell** normally located over the Indian Ocean moves eastward.

The **Walker cell** gets smaller on the South American coast.

west winds

warm surface water

trade winds

Southeast Asia   cold water   South America

evaporation

The absence of monsoon rains causes **droughts** in Indonesia, Australia, and India.

On the eastern side of the Pacific, Peru and Ecuador receive exceptionally abundant **rain**.

The low sea level affects the Australian **coral-reef ecosystems**.

A rise of 7°F to 9°F (4°C to 5°C) in the **temperature** of the water impedes fishing.

The **sea level** rises on the South American coast.

LA NIÑA: THE PENDULUM SWINGS BACK

Each appearance of El Niño is followed by a period called La Niña. Exceptionally strong trade winds cause heavy precipitation in Asia and noticeably cooler water in the eastern Pacific.

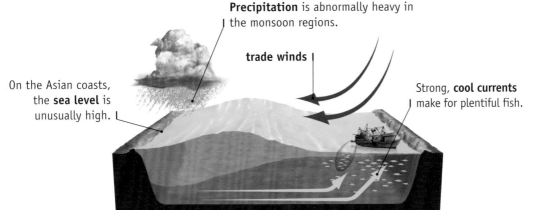

Precipitation is abnormally heavy in the monsoon regions.

trade winds

On the Asian coasts, the **sea level** is unusually high.

Strong, **cool currents** make for plentiful fish.

The Consequences of El Niño and La Niña

A cycle of destruction

On average, El Niño appears every three to seven years in the Pacific Ocean. Its consequences, including floods, hurricanes, droughts, and forest fires, are considerable and affect a large part of the planet. La Niña returns normal conditions to the equatorial Pacific, but amplifies them. It also causes climatic disturbances around the planet, although these upsets are less devastating than El Niño's.

Together, El Niño and La Niña form a relatively regular cycle. By observing the oceans and the atmosphere using satellites and buoys, scientists can easily follow their evolution, but it is not always possible to predict exactly when they will appear.

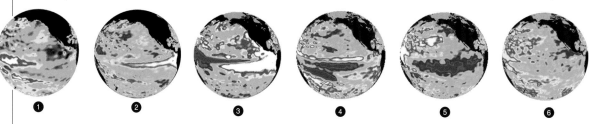

❶　❷　❸　❹　❺　❻

VARIATION IN THE SEA LEVEL COMPARED TO NORMAL (inches)						
−5	−3	−1.5	0	+1.5	+3	+5

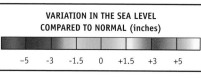

THE CYCLE OVER THE MONTHS

TOPEX/Poseidon, a satellite placed into orbit around Earth at 830 miles (1,330 km) altitude by France and the United States in 1992, measures the height of the oceans around the planet. The radar images of the Pacific Ocean that it gathers are very useful for following the evolution of the El Niño and La Niña phenomena, since an increase in the water's height means that it has become warmer.

In March 1997 ❶, a mass of warm water left Asia and moved toward South America. El Niño was forming. By May ❷, the warm water had reached the South American coast. By the time El Niño reached its maximum extent in November ❸, the California coast was affected, and the sea level was 14 inches (35 cm) above normal near the Galapagos Islands. In June 1998 ❹, the large mass of cold water that began moving from west to east indicated the arrival of La Niña.

In February 1999 ❺, the cold waters of La Niña covered a vast area of the Pacific Ocean. By October of that year ❻, almost all of the Pacific had returned to its normal state.

OBSERVATION BUOYS

With the purpose of reaching a better understanding of El Niño, a major, ongoing study of Pacific atmospheric and oceanic conditions was begun in 1994. Seventy tethered buoys distributed along the equator record data that are then sent by satellite to a laboratory. Sensors on each buoy record surface-water temperature to a depth of about 1,640 feet (500 m), wind direction, atmospheric temperature, and humidity level.

DISASTROUS CLIMATIC CONSEQUENCES

During **El Niño** ❶, the waters of the eastern Pacific are much warmer than usual. This region is influenced by a low pressure system that causes heavy rains, hurricanes, and floods. The southwestern United States, which borders the eastern Pacific, also receives abundant precipitation caused by El Niño. At the same time, the western Pacific is affected by high pressure conditions that considerably reduce the usual rainy monsoon season. Southeast Asia thus suffers drought conditions favorable to forest fires. Many regions of the planet, including Canada, Japan, southeast Australia, Africa, undergo a major rise in atmospheric temperature because of El Niño.

La Niña ❷ brings a general cooling of the atmosphere, particularly in the Far East, western Africa, and western Canada. The southeastern United States, in contrast, gets much warmer and has more frequent hurricanes. The rain intensifies in the western Pacific, Amazonia, and southeast Africa, but becomes scarcer on the Pacific coast of South America.

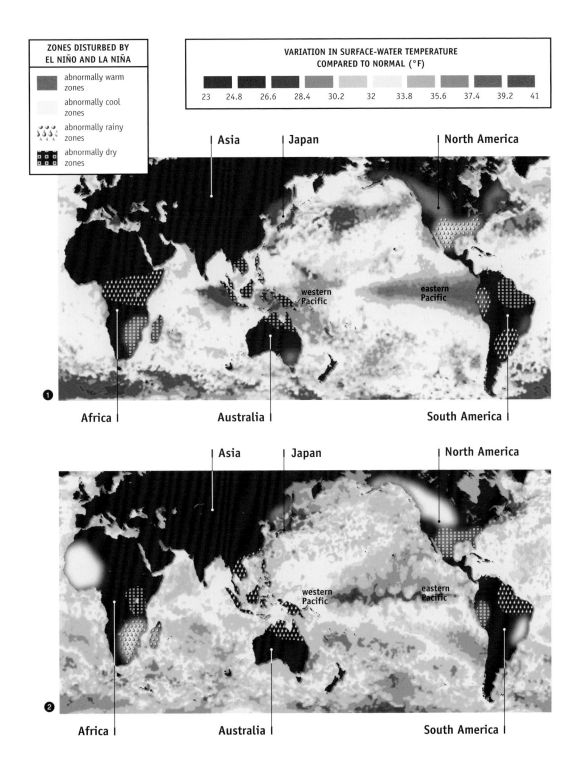

ZONES DISTURBED BY
EL NIÑO AND LA NIÑA

abnormally warm zones

abnormally cool zones

abnormally rainy zones

abnormally dry zones

VARIATION IN SURFACE-WATER TEMPERATURE
COMPARED TO NORMAL (°F)

| 23 | 24.8 | 26.6 | 28.4 | 30.2 | 32 | 33.8 | 35.6 | 37.4 | 39.2 | 41 |

Asia | Japan | North America

western Pacific | eastern Pacific

❶

Africa | Australia | South America

Asia | Japan | North America

western Pacific | eastern Pacific

❷

Africa | Australia | South America

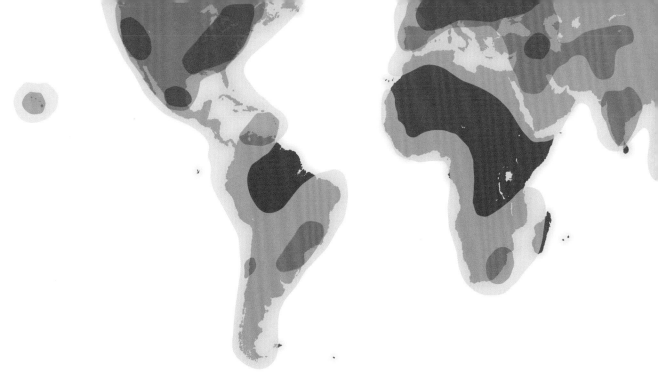

Water, carbon, oxygen, and all materials indispensable to life circulate through different parts of the biosphere. Their tightly interlocked cycles enable matter and energy to be transmitted from one living being to another and from one ecosystem to another. This balance is threatened by many types of pollution: acid rain is damaging the forests, the ozone layer is getting thinner, nitrates are fouling water tables, and nuclear waste that has been buried underground may contaminate the land.

The Environment

The Biosphere

The living world

There are all sorts of hypotheses about life on other planets, none of which has been confirmed by scientific evidence. Earth is still the only planet known to support life. Living organisms exist in many and varied environments that are all distributed through a thin, concentrated layer of earth, water, and air called the biosphere. This habitable part of Earth constitutes a complex community, where animal and plant species live in close relationship with their surroundings and constantly exchange matter and energy with each other.

BETWEEN EARTH, SEA, AND AIR

The biosphere consists of three main physical environments—earth, water, and air—that constantly interact to preserve, reproduce, and develop life. The chemical exchanges that take place between these three elements of the biosphere tend to balance themselves naturally by recycling matter and energy.

The **lithosphere** ❶, which includes the continents, islands, and ocean floor, is the solid outer layer of the planet. Almost all plant species sink their roots into its rock and soil, while a great number of animal species live in contact with it. Some living beings, such as anaerobic bacteria, develop within the ground, while others need air to live.

The **hydrosphere** ❷ is composed of Earth's waters, both saltwater and freshwater, including oceans, rivers, lakes, and underground water. This layer, which partially covers the lithosphere, harbors a great variety of living organisms, from microscopic algae to huge sea mammals.

The **atmosphere** ❸ is the layer of air just above Earth's surface that is very rich in living beings. It also helps to move and disseminate spores, seeds, and microorganisms.

GEOGRAPHIC DIVISIONS OF THE BIOSPHERE: BIOMES

Biomes, or large-scale ecological units, are homogenous communities of living organisms. They are characterized by their plant formations, which are dependent on climatic conditions. Eight biomes, distributed throughout the biosphere, have been identified.

BIOMES

- tundra
- boreal forest
- temperate forest
- temperate grassland
- humid tropical forest
- savanna
- desert
- maquis

HEIGHT OF THE BIOSPHERE

Life is found only within a relatively thin layer of the biosphere; just a little more than 65,600 feet (20,000 m) separate the lowest point of the biosphere, the bottom of the oceans, from the highest point, near the tropopause, or the upper limit of the troposphere.

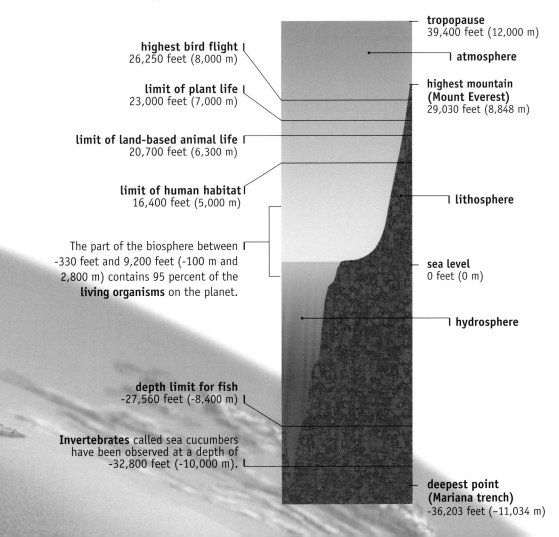

tropopause
39,400 feet (12,000 m)

highest bird flight
26,250 feet (8,000 m)

atmosphere

limit of plant life
23,000 feet (7,000 m)

highest mountain (Mount Everest)
29,030 feet (8,848 m)

limit of land-based animal life
20,700 feet (6,300 m)

limit of human habitat
16,400 feet (5,000 m)

lithosphere

The part of the biosphere between -330 feet and 9,200 feet (-100 m and 2,800 m) contains 95 percent of the **living organisms** on the planet.

sea level
0 feet (0 m)

hydrosphere

depth limit for fish
-27,560 feet (-8,400 m)

Invertebrates called sea cucumbers have been observed at a depth of -32,800 feet (-10,000 m).

deepest point (Mariana trench)
-36,203 feet (-11,034 m)

Ecosystems

Communities of interdependent living beings

Since the energy that it needs to stay alive, move, and reproduce comes from the food it eats—and the food it eats comes from other animals and plants—no animal can live isolated from other species. The ecological grouping of animals and plants living in interrelation in a given environment is called an ecosystem. This basic unit of the biosphere can be as small as a wall of stones and as vast as an ocean. An ecosystem is kept in equilibrium by the presence of each of its components in a food chain, where they are producers and consumers of energy.

LIVING BEINGS IN THEIR ENVIRONMENT

An ecosystem is defined mainly by its biotope—its physical environment, climate, and distribution of species—and the group of living organisms that populate it, including animals, plants, and decomposers, which are called its biocoenosis. These two elements are tightly linked; the different aspects (geological, climatic, geographic, chemical, etc.) of the biotope determine the composition and diversity of the biocoenosis, which, in turn, influences the environment and can even change it radically.

Ecosystems are extremely varied in size. A lake, for example, is an ecosystem, and so is the Amazon forest. In spite of its homogeneity, an ecosystem is never a totally closed system. Fed by solar energy, it constantly exchanges mineral and organic substances with nearby systems.

Although it is a self-contained ecosystem, a **lake** is in constant contact with the surrounding environment. Land-based animals visit it to drink, feed, or reproduce.

Debris that makes up sediments deposited at the bottom of a lake come from the **plants** that grow on its border.

Insect larvae and **microorganisms** develop in a lake's mud, on its bottom, and on its shores.

Chlorophyllous plants form the base of the aquatic food chain. They also help to enrich the water with oxygen.

Fish make up the **permanent fauna** of a lake.

A number of factors, including temperature, acidity, oxygen content, and quantity of available light, influence the development of **aquatic life**.

TRANSMISSION OF ENERGY THROUGH THE FOOD CHAIN

Food is the main source of the energy transmitted from one species to another in an ecosystem. The food chain transports matter and the energy it contains to increasingly complex living beings. At the same time, corpses of dead creatures and excrement from all living creatures in the ecosystem are decomposed by microorganisms.

A great quantity of energy, however, escapes the food chain. When an animal is eaten, only 10 percent of the energy that it took in during its life is transmitted, as it used the rest to stay alive. This energy loss explains why a food chain rarely has more than four or five links.

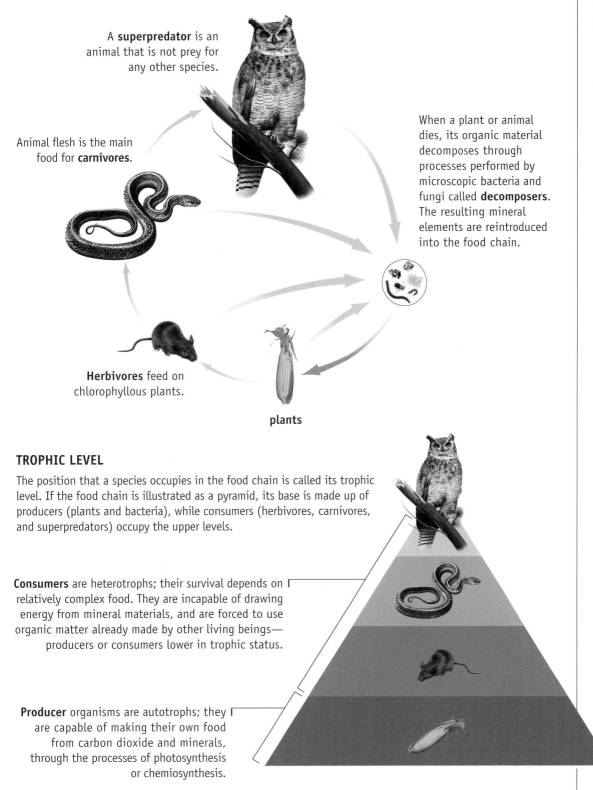

A **superpredator** is an animal that is not prey for any other species.

Animal flesh is the main food for **carnivores**.

When a plant or animal dies, its organic material decomposes through processes performed by microscopic bacteria and fungi called **decomposers**. The resulting mineral elements are reintroduced into the food chain.

Herbivores feed on chlorophyllous plants.

plants

TROPHIC LEVEL

The position that a species occupies in the food chain is called its trophic level. If the food chain is illustrated as a pyramid, its base is made up of producers (plants and bacteria), while consumers (herbivores, carnivores, and superpredators) occupy the upper levels.

Consumers are heterotrophs; their survival depends on relatively complex food. They are incapable of drawing energy from mineral materials, and are forced to use organic matter already made by other living beings—producers or consumers lower in trophic status.

Producer organisms are autotrophs; they are capable of making their own food from carbon dioxide and minerals, through the processes of photosynthesis or chemiosynthesis.

Soil

Far from being a dead environment, the ground is crawling with life. Scientists estimate that about 35 cubic feet (one cubic meter) of fertile soil harbors nearly one billion living organisms. The important biological, chemical, and physical processes that take place in the soil have led edaphologists, or scientists who study the soil, to consider it a true ecosystem.

PEDOGENESIS

The formation of soil, known as pedogenesis, has three phases. First, water that has infiltrated the rock splits it apart by gelifraction, which produces a layer of rocky fragments called **regolith ❶**. The living organisms that penetrate into the cracks in the regolith gradually create a thin layer of partially decomposed organic debris. This **skeletal soil ❷** enables grasses and small shrubs to grow. It takes about 10,000 years for the early skeletal soil to become **mature soil ❸**, which allows an exchange between the various soil layers. In mature soil, looser earth and water infiltrate ❹ between the rocky fragments, which migrate ❺ toward the surface.

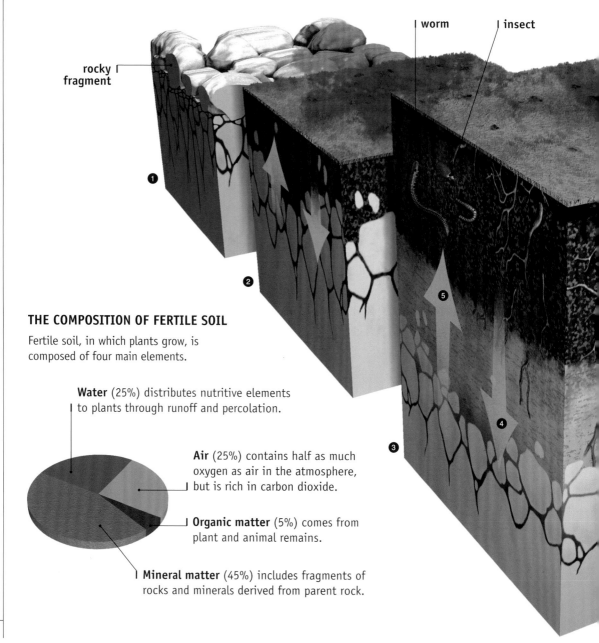

worm

insect

rocky fragment

THE COMPOSITION OF FERTILE SOIL

Fertile soil, in which plants grow, is composed of four main elements.

Water (25%) distributes nutritive elements to plants through runoff and percolation.

Air (25%) contains half as much oxygen as air in the atmosphere, but is rich in carbon dioxide.

Organic matter (5%) comes from plant and animal remains.

Mineral matter (45%) includes fragments of rocks and minerals derived from parent rock.

LIFE IN THE SOIL

Many animals, such as worms, insects, and small mammals, dig into, work in, aerate, and enrich the soil. The soil also contains many types of algae, fungi, and bacteria, microorganisms that decompose organic matter into minerals and, thus, provide nourishment for plants.

algae

bacterium

fungus

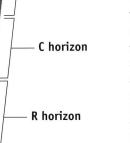

O horizon

A horizon

mammal

B horizon

C horizon

R horizon

parent rock

SOIL TYPES

The nature of the rocky mantle, also known as parent rock, largely determines the type of soil above it.

 Heavy and often humid, **clay soil** is characterized by small particles about .00008 inch (.002 mm) in diameter.

Sandy soil is dry and aerated, not very fertile, and made of relatively large particles of up to .08 inch (2 mm).

 Limestone soil is composed mostly of stones. It contains much calcium and potassium.

Spongy and rich in organic matter, **peaty soil** easily retains humidity.

 Silty soil, with its very tiny particles of between .000008 and .00008 inch (.0002 and .002 mm), is soft to the touch.

HORIZONS

The different layers of the soil are called horizons. The top layer, or **0 horizon**, is composed of bits of dead leaves, twigs, and animal remains, known as humus. The **A horizon**, formed of plant roots, living organisms, and minerals, is arable. The layer below, in which minerals and clay from the top layer gather, is called **B horizon**, or the accumulation layer. Known as **C horizon**, the subsoil, or weathering, layer contains fragmented rocks from the lower layer. The lowest layer of soil, **R horizon**, is made mainly of parent rock from the rocky mantle.

The Water Cycle

Constant circulation between sea, sky, and land

Every year, about 120,670 cubic miles (502,800 cubic kilometers) of water—the equivalent of a layer over 4.5 feet (1.4 m) thick—evaporates from the oceans. The sea level does not drop, however, because the oceans are continually fed by precipitation and runoff from rivers. This global circulation plays an essential role in the redistribution of water around the planet.

FROM OCEAN TO OCEAN

The heat of solar rays ❶ is responsible for the evaporation of the top layer of the oceans ❷. Lighter than air, water vapor rises ❸ until it meets colder air, which causes it to condense and form clouds ❹. Most of the water contained in clouds returns to the ocean in the form of rain ❺. Pushed by winds ❻, some clouds float over landmasses, on which they drop their precipitation ❼. When their water reaches Earth's surface, it either runs off to form streams and rivers ❽ or sinks into the soil and infiltrates to the subsoil ❾. Plants draw water from the subsoil and transform it into vapor through transpiration ❿. The surplus of infiltrated water feeds slow-flowing underground rivers, which impregnate the rock and form the water table ⓫. This underground water reappears at the surface as it feeds watercourses such as lakes and rivers ⓬. These bodies of water partially evaporate ⓭ due to the action of the Sun, while flowing ⓮ toward the oceans. Finally, some water from the subsoil flows directly back to the ocean ⓯.

precipitation

Oceans cover two-thirds of Earth's surface.

DISTRIBUTION OF WATER

The total quantity of water on Earth is estimated at over 326 million cubic miles (1.36 billion km³). It is distributed between the oceans, fresh water bodies such as ice sheets, lakes, underground water, and rivers, and atmospheric water vapor.

oceans (95.5%)

atmosphere (.001%)

fresh water (4.5%)

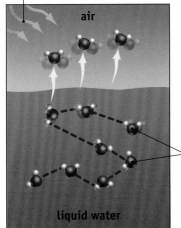

solar energy

air

water molecules

liquid water

EVAPORATION

The electrical charge in each water molecule creates a mutual attraction between them. When the molecules are in a liquid state, they move slowly and remain linked to each other. Solar energy increases the speed of the surface molecules, causing their links to break and the molecules to rise into the air. In this way, water evaporates.

An **impermeable layer** keeps infiltrating water from penetrating deeper into Earth.

The **water table** is a layer of rocks saturated with water.

THE ROLE OF PLANTS

The roots of a plant suck water from the soil and combine it with mineral salts so the plant can absorb water more easily. The plant then eliminates the water by transpiration through its stomata, the tiny openings on the undersides of its leaves. Each year, a forest transpires a quantity of water vapor equal to a layer of water 4 feet (1.2 m) deep over its area.

The Carbon and Oxygen Cycles

Continuous interactions

Carbon and oxygen are indispensable to life. They are closely linked through various interactions, and their biological, geological, and chemical cycles continually circulate matter, which enables life to be perpetuated. Both elements are naturally present in our atmosphere, but in unequal quantities. Oxygen (O_2) constitutes 21 percent of air, while carbon dioxide (CO_2) constitutes just .036 percent. Carbon, on the other hand, is abundant in sedimentary rocks, combustible fuels, the oceans, and the biomass.

An essential component of the atmosphere, **oxygen** (O_2) comes mainly from photosynthesis performed by chlorophyllous plants.

Water enters the air through **evaporation**. In the upper atmosphere, molecules of water vapor (H_2O) can be dissociated by the Sun's ultraviolet rays. This process increases the quantity of atmospheric oxygen.

The oceans receive carbon from the **dissolution** of carbon dioxide in the atmosphere and the erosion of sedimentary rocks such as limestone and chalk.

PHOTOSYNTHESIS AND RESPIRATION

Green plants contribute to the carbon and oxygen cycles through two types of reactions. **Photosynthesis** Ⓐ occurs only when a green plant is exposed to light. In this process, plants use carbon dioxide from the atmosphere to make organic materials such as sugars, lipids, and protids. The process also releases oxygen. Plant **respiration** Ⓑ, which takes place day and night, is similar to respiration in animals; plants absorb oxygen and expel carbon dioxide.

Ⓐ

Ⓑ

→ carbon dioxide
→ oxygen

CARBON IN THE FOOD CHAIN

Carbon dioxide (CO_2) ❶ contained in the atmosphere is consumed by chlorophyllous plants ❷, which transform carbon through photosynthesis into a form usable to produce living matter. Animals ❸ assimilate this plant matter by digesting it and then expel carbon dioxide as part of their respiratory processes. Decomposers such as bacteria and fungi degrade animal dung and dead biomass ❹, also releasing carbon dioxide into the atmosphere in the process.

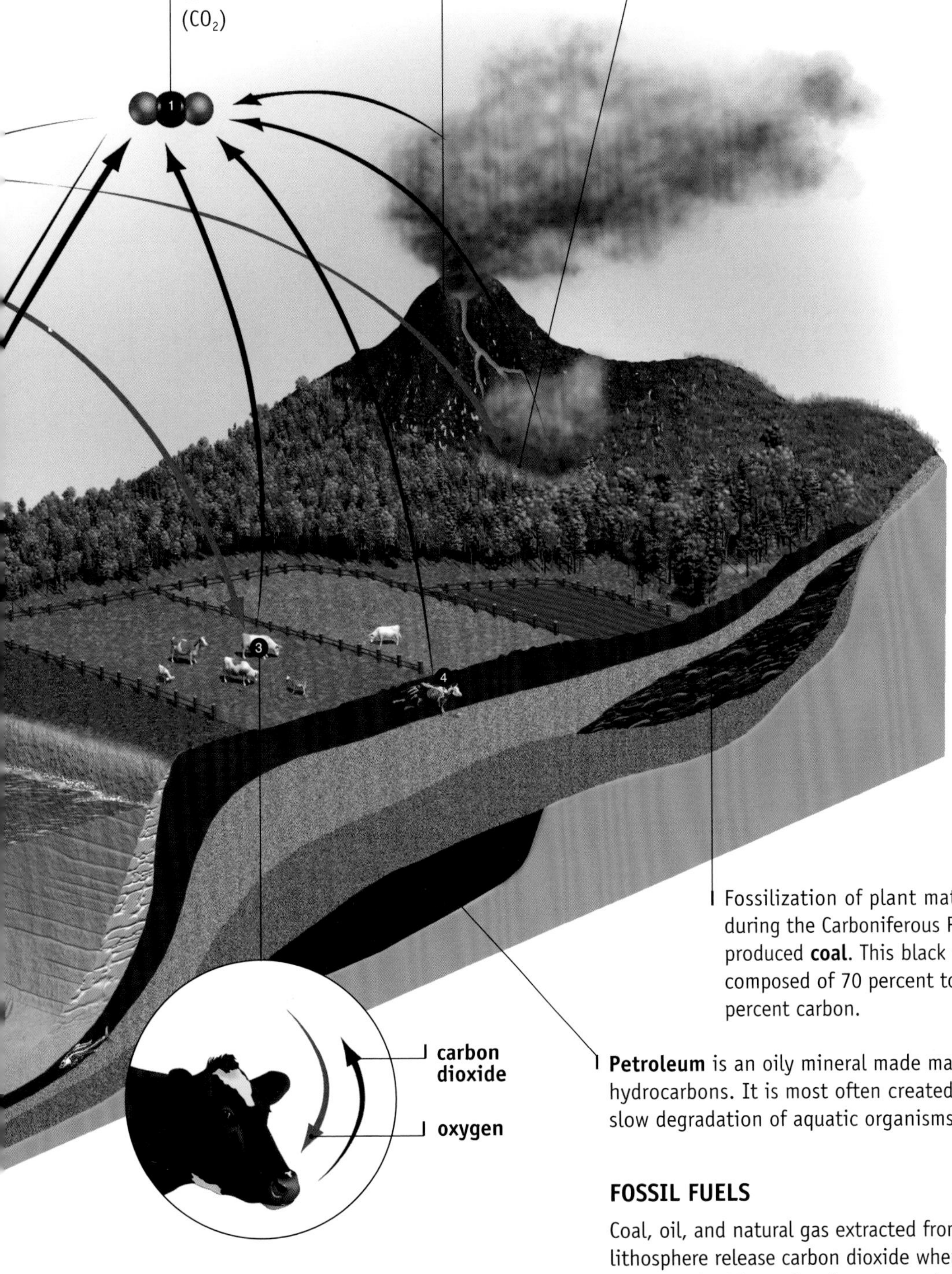

Volcanic eruptions release carbon dioxide into the atmosphere.

carbon dioxide (CO_2)

Like all forms of combustion, **forest fires** consume oxygen and produce carbon dioxide.

Fossilization of plant matter during the Carboniferous Period produced **coal**. This black rock is composed of 70 percent to 95 percent carbon.

carbon dioxide

oxygen

Petroleum is an oily mineral made mainly of hydrocarbons. It is most often created by the slow degradation of aquatic organisms.

FOSSIL FUELS

Coal, oil, and natural gas extracted from the lithosphere release carbon dioxide when they are burned. This combustion puts carbon that was stored in rocks for several hundred million years back into circulation in the atmosphere.

Animal respiration is a form of combustion; it uses oxygen to burn sugars, and it releases carbon dioxide into the atmosphere.

The Phosphorus and Nitrogen Cycles

Transformation, then assimilation

Phosphorus and nitrogen are essential nutrients for living beings. Although they are present in large quantities on Earth, they are not absorbed directly but through intermediary components that circulate between different environments and are parts of food chains.

THE PHOSPHORUS CYCLE

Phosphorus is a very widespread element on Earth, but it does not exist in its pure state in the atmosphere. On the other hand, it is naturally present in the form of phosphates ❶ in the parent rock. Erosion causes broken up phosphates to enter the soil ❷, where they can be absorbed by plants ❸. The plants combine the phosphorus with various components to make living matter that is eaten by herbivores ❹ and, eventually, by carnivores ❺ through the food chain. Microorganisms decompose animal dung and dead organisms ❻. This process returns the phosphorus to the soil, where it can once again be assimilated by other plants.

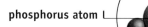

phosphorus atom

oxygen atom

A phosphate is a chemical composite formed by the union of a **phosphate ion** with other metallic ions, such as magnesium, calcium, sodium, or potassium.

Phosphate particles carried by the wind sometimes remain in suspension in the atmosphere until **precipitation** brings them back to Earth's surface.

Phosphorus is indispensable to **living beings**, since it is used in the composition of DNA, the main constituent of chromosomes.

soil

When phosphates are deposited in the ocean, they become part of the sediment on the ocean floor. Over several million years, geologic movements can bring these sedimentary **phosphates** to the surface of the soil.

THE NITROGEN CYCLE

Although it is very abundant in Earth's atmosphere, gaseous nitrogen (N_2) ❶ cannot be assimilated directly by living beings. It must first be fixed in a mineral form through combination with other chemical elements. These transformations are sometimes produced in the atmosphere by the action of solar radiation, combustion, or thunderbolts, but usually microorganisms ❷ fix the nitrogen in the soil by producing ammonium and nitrate ions. Plants ❸ can then absorb the nitrogen and use it to make amino acids, the basic constituents of proteins. This organic nitrogen is transmitted to animals ❹ through the food chain. Certain microorganisms ❺ transform the organic nitrogen contained in excrement and dead organisms into mineral nitrogen, then into gaseous nitrogen through a denitrification reaction, and the cycle starts again.

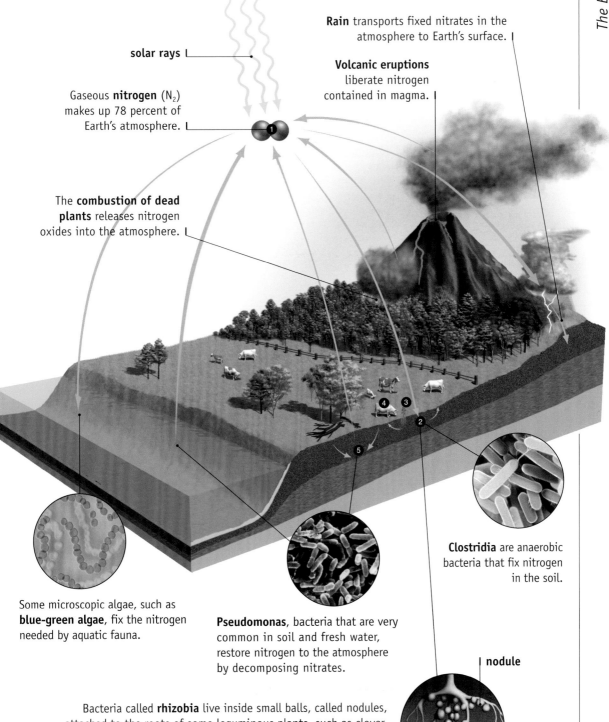

Rain transports fixed nitrates in the atmosphere to Earth's surface.

solar rays

Volcanic eruptions liberate nitrogen contained in magma.

Gaseous **nitrogen** (N_2) makes up 78 percent of Earth's atmosphere.

The **combustion of dead plants** releases nitrogen oxides into the atmosphere.

Clostridia are anaerobic bacteria that fix nitrogen in the soil.

Some microscopic algae, such as **blue-green algae**, fix the nitrogen needed by aquatic fauna.

Pseudomonas, bacteria that are very common in soil and fresh water, restore nitrogen to the atmosphere by decomposing nitrates.

nodule

Bacteria called **rhizobia** live inside small balls, called nodules, attached to the roots of some leguminous plants, such as clover. By synthesizing ammonium ions, they supply the plant with the nitrogen it needs and enrich the soil.

clover

The Greenhouse Effect

A heat trap

Certain gases in the atmosphere are able to absorb the infrared rays emitted by Earth. This natural phenomenon, called the greenhouse effect, helps to maintain a temperature conducive to life on the planet. Without it, in fact, the average temperature at the surface of Earth, which is 59°F (15°C), would be no higher than −.4°F (−18°C). Life on Earth as we know it would be impossible. By emitting increasing amounts of greenhouse gases into the atmosphere, certain human activities are amplifying this phenomenon and, many scientists believe, helping to increase the planet's temperature.

THE NATURAL GREENHOUSE EFFECT

Only half of the Sun's rays directly reach Earth's surface; the rest are reflected back into space or absorbed by clouds and the tropopause. The ground absorbs the rays it receives and transforms them into infrared rays, which it then emits into the atmosphere. However, water vapor and certain other atmospheric gases, called greenhouse gases, block some of these rays and turn them back toward Earth. Since infrared radiation transports thermal energy, this phenomenon increases the temperature of the ambient air. The increase in temperature as a result of the reflection of infrared rays back toward Earth is called the greenhouse effect.

solar rays

Atmospheric gases above the **troposphere** absorb and reflect 5 percent of solar rays.

Some **heat** escapes toward the upper atmosphere, since not all of the infrared rays are blocked.

Clouds absorb 20 percent of solar rays and reflect another 22 percent of them back toward the sun.

Earth's **surface** absorbs most of the solar radiation that reaches it, reflecting only 3 percent of it back toward the upper layers of the atmosphere.

infrared rays

Clouds return some infrared rays toward the ground.

Water vapor and **greenhouse gases** capture some of the infrared rays that Earth has emitted and return them to the surface.

GREENHOUSE GASES

Greenhouse gases are gaseous substances that contribute to the heating of the atmosphere by capturing infrared rays. Some of these gases, such as carbon dioxide, methane, and nitrous oxide, are naturally present in the atmosphere, while others, such as CFCs (chlorofluorocarbons), are the result of human activity. Whatever their origin, the concentration of greenhouse gases has constantly grown since the beginning of the Industrial Revolution, in the mid-19th century.

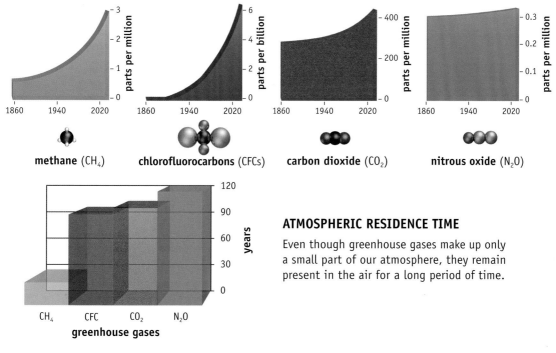

methane (CH_4) chlorofluorocarbons (CFCs) carbon dioxide (CO_2) nitrous oxide (N_2O)

ATMOSPHERIC RESIDENCE TIME

Even though greenhouse gases make up only a small part of our atmosphere, they remain present in the air for a long period of time.

greenhouse gases

THE GROWING GREENHOUSE EFFECT

Many human activities increase the concentration of greenhouse gases in the atmosphere. Factory farming uses fertilizers that liberate more nitrous oxide, and the digestive systems of ruminants produce methane. Air conditioning systems use CFCs. Fires and motor vehicles release carbon monoxide, as do factories that burn fossil fuels such as coal, natural gas, and fuel oil. Greenhouse gases are more and more abundant, sending great amounts of infrared rays back toward Earth's surface.

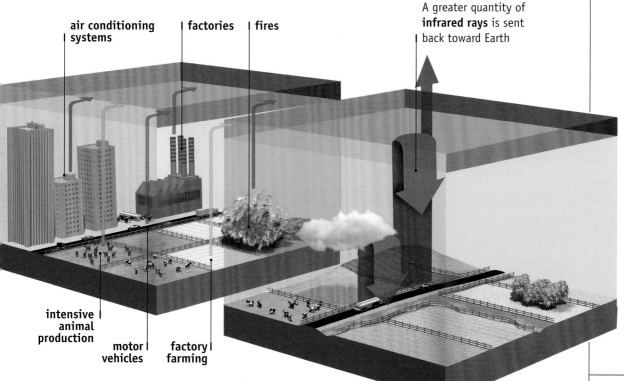

air conditioning systems | factories | fires

A greater quantity of **infrared rays** is sent back toward Earth

intensive animal production

motor vehicles | factory farming

Global Warming

Unpredictable climatic upsets

Greenhouse gases have been increasing in concentration in the lower atmosphere for a century and a half. According to many studies, this phenomenon is directly responsible for the current warming of the planet, which could become even more intense. The complexity and diversity of factors at play—including winds, ocean currents, ice, clouds, plants, and the greenhouse effect—make the consequences of such a climatic change difficult to predict. They could be anything from benign to disastrous.

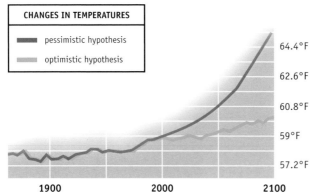

CHANGES IN TEMPERATURES

— pessimistic hypothesis

— optimistic hypothesis

64.4°F
62.6°F
60.8°F
59°F
57.2°F

1900   2000   2100

RISING TEMPERATURES

The last years of the 20th century were the hottest since the Middle Ages. The average annual temperature at Earth's surface has risen by a little over 1°F (.6°C) in the past century, and studies indicate that it could climb another 1.8°F (1°C) to 5.4°F (3°C) in the next 100 years if greenhouse gas emissions continue to increase at the current rate. Earth would then be as warm as it was 100,000 years ago.

POSSIBLE CONSEQUENCES OF GLOBAL WARMING

If temperatures dramatically increase, many Eurasian and North American areas, such as **Alaska**, may receive greater precipitation.

The droughts that may affect the southwestern **United States, Mexico, and Central America** if Earth's temperatures rise could have a major effect on the agricultural output of these regions.

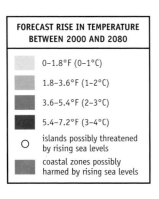

FORECAST RISE IN TEMPERATURE BETWEEN 2000 AND 2080

0–1.8°F (0–1°C)

1.8–3.6°F (1–2°C)

3.6–5.4°F (2–3°C)

5.4–7.2°F (3–4°C)

○ islands possibly threatened by rising sea levels

coastal zones possibly harmed by rising sea levels

○ Bahamas

○○○ Lesser Antilles

Tampa

Miami ●

If global temperatures rise significantly, **Florida** would be threatened by a rise in sea level, and it also would be affected by a larger number of hurricanes.

FLOODING OF COASTAL ZONES

Sea level could rise by over 31 inches (80 centimeters) during the 21st century. Several thousand inhabited islands, especially in the Caribbean Sea and the Indian and Pacific oceans, would be partially submerged. Many coastal regions—for example, those in Florida, the Netherlands, West Africa, and China—and the great river deltas would also be threatened by the sea's advance.

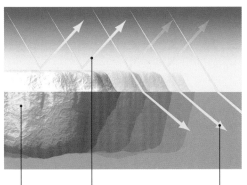

MELTING OF THE PACK ICE

Between 1970 and 2000, the Arctic pack ice lost more than 10 percent of its area, dropping from 5.2 to 4.6 million square miles (13.5 to 12 million km²). It has also become thinner. Although the melting of ocean ice does not cause the sea level to rise, it does allow the water to absorb more solar rays, which intensifies global warming. Arctic regions may see a much greater increase in temperature than the rest of the planet.

| pack ice | solar rays reflected by the ice | solar rays absorbed by the ocean |

RISING TEMPERATURES, RISING WATER LEVELS

Earth's climatic balance is so fragile that a very slight variation in temperature can have considerable consequences, but it is difficult to predict their extent. A rise in the average water level is the most commonly predicted consequence. It could result from the combination of two factors: the melting of the Antarctic and Greenland icecaps, and, especially, the thermal expansion of the water. Among the possible effects are intensification of droughts, disappearance of the tundra, weakening of the Gulf Stream, increase in the number of hurricanes, and spreading of diseases such as malaria.

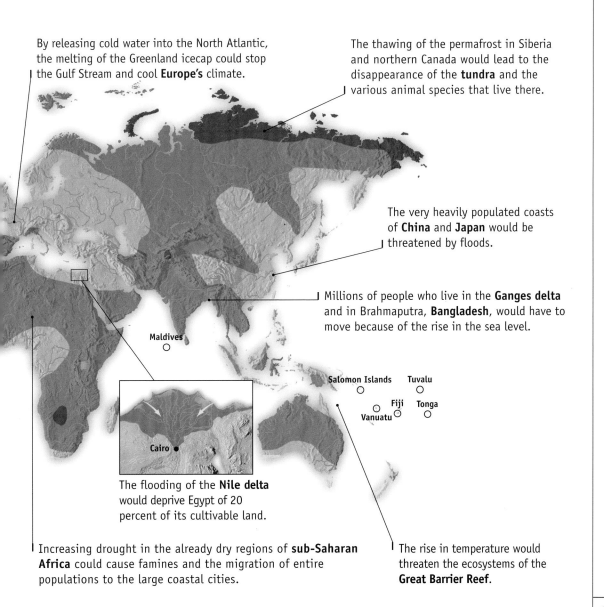

By releasing cold water into the North Atlantic, the melting of the Greenland icecap could stop the Gulf Stream and cool **Europe's** climate.

The thawing of the permafrost in Siberia and northern Canada would lead to the disappearance of the **tundra** and the various animal species that live there.

The very heavily populated coasts of **China** and **Japan** would be threatened by floods.

Millions of people who live in the **Ganges delta** and in Brahmaputra, **Bangladesh**, would have to move because of the rise in the sea level.

Maldives ○

Salomon Islands ○ Tuvalu ○

Vanuatu ○ Fiji ○ Tonga ○

The flooding of the **Nile delta** would deprive Egypt of 20 percent of its cultivable land.

Cairo ●

Increasing drought in the already dry regions of **sub-Saharan Africa** could cause famines and the migration of entire populations to the large coastal cities.

The rise in temperature would threaten the ecosystems of the **Great Barrier Reef**.

The Ozone Layer

A fragile filter

Ozone (O_3) is a bluish gas whose molecules are composed of three oxygen atoms. It is found mainly in the stratosphere at altitudes of between 12.5 and 18.5 miles (20 and 30 km). This region of relatively high ozone concentration is known as the ozone layer.

Even though its concentration is only 10 parts per million, the ozone layer acts as a shield for Earth against the Sun's ultraviolet rays. Without this filter, solar rays could cause skin cancer in living cells, affecting all levels of the food chain. The thinning of the ozone layer, revealed by satellites, is a disturbing phenomenon caused by the release of industrial products such as CFCs into the atmosphere.

NATURAL FORMATION AND DESTRUCTION OF OZONE

An ozone molecule forms naturally in the stratosphere when an ultraviolet ray ❶ from the Sun hits an oxygen molecule (O_2) ❷ and decomposes it into two oxygen atoms. Each of these two atoms can join another oxygen molecule ❸ and create an ozone molecule (O_3) ❹. When ozone absorbs ultraviolet light ❺, it uses the energy to split into an oxygen molecule ❻ and a free atom ❼. The free atom can come into contact with another ozone molecule ❽ and form two oxygen molecules ❾. This process normally reaches a balance in which generation and destruction of ozone are equal.

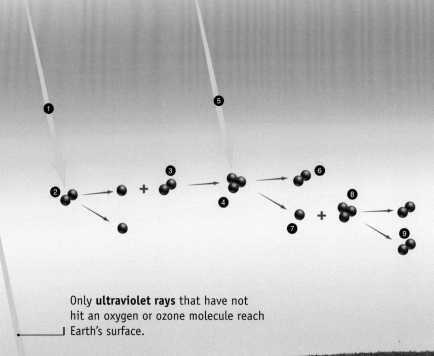

Only **ultraviolet rays** that have not hit an oxygen or ozone molecule reach Earth's surface.

DEPLETION OF THE OZONE LAYER

Several satellites are used to measure the thickness of the ozone layer. Images synthesized from satellite observations show that it is slowly growing thinner all around Earth. Every spring since 1984, a "hole" in the ozone layer—actually a lessening of ozone concentration—has been forming and then disappearing over a 4- to 6-week period above Antarctica. On the Dobson scale, which is used to indicate the thickness of the ozone layer, each 100 units corresponds to about .04 inch (1 mm) of compressed ozone.

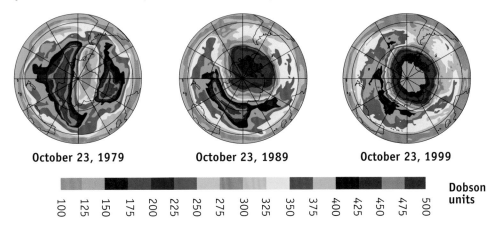

October 23, 1979   **October 23, 1989**   **October 23, 1999**

| 100 | 125 | 150 | 175 | 200 | 225 | 250 | 275 | 300 | 325 | 350 | 375 | 400 | 425 | 450 | 475 | 500 |

Dobson units

THE EFFECT OF CFCs ON THE STRATOSPHERE

When an ultraviolet ray **1** from the Sun hits a CFC molecule **2**, it liberates a chlorine atom **3**. This chlorine atom can then combine with an ozone molecule (O_3) **4** to produce an oxygen (O_2) molecule **5** and a chlorine monoxide (ClO) molecule **6**. If a chlorine monoxide molecule meets a free oxygen atom **7**, their reaction produces an oxygen molecule **8** and a chlorine atom **9**, which is free to destroy another ozone molecule. It is estimated that this chain reaction can be repeated up to 100,000 times before the chlorine atom combines with other chemicals and is no longer able to participate in ozone-destroying reactions.

Chlorofluorocarbons (CFCs) are humanmade gases used in insulators, refrigeration systems, and aerosol spray cans.

When they are not absorbed by ozone molecules, greater numbers of **ultraviolet rays** reach Earth's surface.

Sources of Air Pollution

How humans foul the air

The atmosphere, 99 percent of which is made up of nitrogen and oxygen, has retained a remarkably stable composition for millions of years. The concentrations of certain of its components, however, have undergone considerable variations over the last two centuries. Human activities are largely responsible for this transformation, the medium- and long-term effects of which are not yet known.

In tropical regions, controlled **forest fires** are often used to clear new land for cultivation. This practice liberates carbon monoxide, methane, and nitrous oxide.

Some polluting gases react with solar radiation to form ozone. This reaction is part of the process by which **smog** is formed.

When nitric fertilizers are used on the soil, **agriculture** leads to the production of nitrous oxide.

Rice paddies release large quantities of methane into the atmosphere.

In **landfill sites**, the decomposition of organic matter produces methane.

Anaerobic bacteria present in the digestive tracts of ruminants produce methane, which makes **cattle farming** a major source of this greenhouse gas.

All living beings expel carbon dioxide, but only plants are able to use it for photosynthesis, the process by which they feed themselves with the help of the Sun. Large-scale **deforestation**, thus, leads to more of this gas in the atmosphere.

ATMOSPHERIC POLLUTANTS

Polluting gases and particles make up only a tiny part of the atmosphere. Most of them have some natural origins such as volcanoes, forest fires, and decomposition processes. Development of industrial activities over the last two centuries, however, has considerably increased their concentration. Some composites, such as chlorofluorocarbons (CFCs), did not exist in the atmosphere 100 years ago.

Among the polluting gases, sulfur dioxide (SO_2) is involved in acid rain. Nitrogen oxide (NO) and nitrogen dioxide (NO_2) are involved both in acid rain and in smog formation. CFCs are the main substance responsible for the damage to the ozone layer, and they also play a part in the greenhouse effect, along with methane (CH_4), carbon dioxide (CO_2), and nitrous oxide (N_2O).

Nongaseous air pollution takes many forms, including coarse particles such as coal soot and dust; small metallic particles of lead, copper, zinc, or cadmium; and very fine salt particles called nitrates and sulfates. This form of air pollution is particularly threatening to health.

Winds transport atmospheric pollutants to other regions, where they fall in the form of **acid rain**.

industrial waste

INDUSTRIAL POLLUTION

Heavy industry produces a huge amount of air pollution. Coal-powered electric power plants release very large quantities of sulfur dioxide and nitrogen oxide, while metallurgic plants release particles of many heavy metals. Many other pollutants are produced by specialized industries, including fluorine, produced by aluminum and glass plants; vinyl chloride, a byproduct of plastics processing; hydrochloric acid, made by incineration plants; and mercaptan, produced by paper plants.

Since gasoline engines emit carbon monoxide, nitrogen oxide, sulfur dioxide, and hydrocarbons, **automobile traffic** is one of the main causes of air pollution. Motor vehicles are responsible for a total of one-third of all polluting gases emitted.

Some **household appliances and products**, such as refrigerators, air conditioners, and aerosol sprays, release chlorofluorocarbons (CFCs). Combustion heating systems emit carbon monoxide.

The Effects of Air Pollution

A worldwide problem

Smog in large cities, acid rain, thinning of the ozone layer, amplification of the greenhouse effect—air pollution has many effects, and they are not limited to industrial regions. Air currents disperse pollutants over every continent, sometimes very far from the source of the pollution. Lead pollution has even been found in the coats of polar bears.

Europe

California

east coast of
North America

Baku

Mexico City

New Delhi

Caracas

AIR POLLUTION AROUND THE WORLD

Emissions of pollution, due mainly to motor vehicles and industry, are concentrated in the Northern Hemisphere, especially in three zones: the United States (east coast, California), Europe (including Russia and the Baku region), and the Far East (Japan, Korea, Shanghai region). Secondary pollution zones are appearing around the industrial metropolises of other countries: Mexico City, Mexico; São Paulo, Brazil; Caracas, Venezuela; Johannesburg, South Africa; the island nation of Singapore; and New Delhi, India.

São Paulo

Johannesburg

POLLUTION EMISSIONS

- heavy
- average
- low
- very low

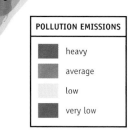

WHERE DO POLLUTANTS LAND?

Most pollutants fall to Earth near their source in the form of dry deposits ❶. The rest, carried by the wind ❷, drift for several hundred miles (km) before falling to the ground due to precipitation ❸. When they reach high altitudes ❹, some polluting gases may be transported by the wind and deposited ❺ thousands of miles (km) from their place of origin. CFCs reach the stratosphere ❻, where they contribute to the depletion of the ozone layer.

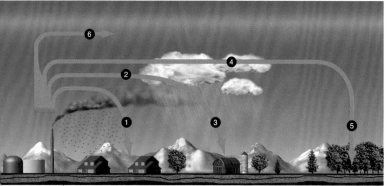

DISPERSION OF NORTH AMERICAN POLLUTION

Pollution emitted into the atmosphere in the northeastern United States and eastern Canada is dispersed by surface winds. Most pollution is deposited near its source. Some of these gases, however, are carried by high-altitude winds over the Atlantic Ocean and even into western Europe.

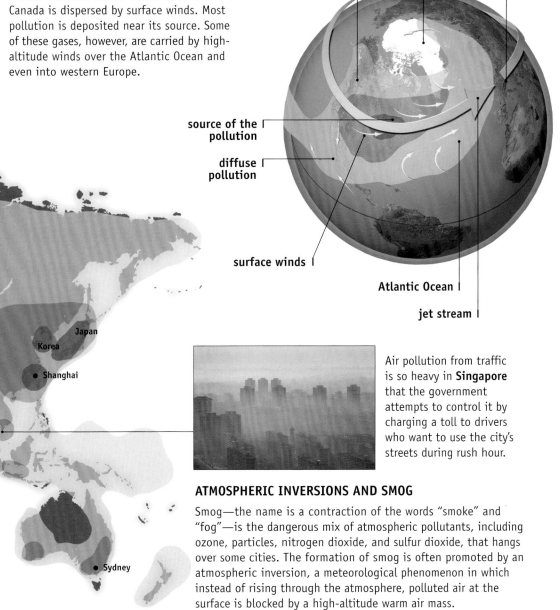

North Pole

North America

Europe

source of the pollution

diffuse pollution

surface winds

Atlantic Ocean

jet stream

Japan

Korea

Shanghai

Sydney

Air pollution from traffic is so heavy in **Singapore** that the government attempts to control it by charging a toll to drivers who want to use the city's streets during rush hour.

ATMOSPHERIC INVERSIONS AND SMOG

Smog—the name is a contraction of the words "smoke" and "fog"—is the dangerous mix of atmospheric pollutants, including ozone, particles, nitrogen dioxide, and sulfur dioxide, that hangs over some cities. The formation of smog is often promoted by an atmospheric inversion, a meteorological phenomenon in which instead of rising through the atmosphere, polluted air at the surface is blocked by a high-altitude warm air mass.

When a coastal city is located near a mountain, the mountain may impede air movement. Trapped by an atmospheric inversion and pushed inland by the sea breeze, the polluted air cannot escape toward the interior. This situation prevails in Los Angeles in the summer.

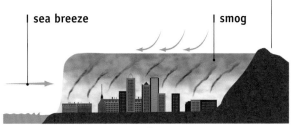

sea breeze

smog

coastal smog

A city located in a valley or basin, such as London, England, can become smoggy if its winter is humid. Clouds keep solar rays from warming the surface air, so it stays cold, humid, and polluted, which maintains and increases the smog phenomenon.

valley smog

Acid Rain

When rain becomes toxic

Rainwater is naturally acidic (pH 5.6), since air contains carbon dioxide (CO_2), which is transformed into carbonic acid when it comes into contact with water as it falls from a cloud. Industrial pollution, however, increases this acidity. Effects of this type of pollution were observed in Pitlochry, Scotland, in 1974, where rain was as acidic as lemon juice—1,000 times more acidic than normal rain. Acid rain has disastrous effects on the environment, especially on forests and lakes.

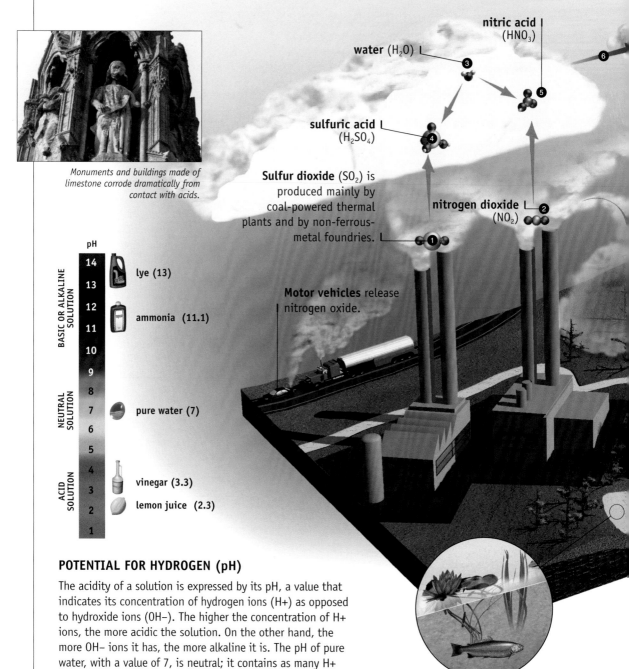

Monuments and buildings made of limestone corrode dramatically from contact with acids.

nitric acid (HNO_3)

water (H_2O)

sulfuric acid (H_2SO_4)

Sulfur dioxide (SO_2) is produced mainly by coal-powered thermal plants and by non-ferrous-metal foundries.

nitrogen dioxide (NO_2)

Motor vehicles release nitrogen oxide.

pH scale

pH		
BASIC OR ALKALINE SOLUTION	14	lye (13)
	13	
	12	ammonia (11.1)
	11	
	10	
	9	
NEUTRAL SOLUTION	8	
	7	pure water (7)
	6	
	5	
ACID SOLUTION	4	vinegar (3.3)
	3	
	2	lemon juice (2.3)
	1	

POTENTIAL FOR HYDROGEN (pH)

The acidity of a solution is expressed by its pH, a value that indicates its concentration of hydrogen ions (H+) as opposed to hydroxide ions (OH–). The higher the concentration of H+ ions, the more acidic the solution. On the other hand, the more OH– ions it has, the more alkaline it is. The pH of pure water, with a value of 7, is neutral; it contains as many H+ ions as it does OH– ions. The pH scale, which runs from 1 to 14, is logarithmic—that is, each whole value corresponds to a concentration 10 times higher than the preceding whole value. Thus, lemon juice (pH 2.3) is 10 times more acidic than vinegar (pH 3.3), while lye (pH 13) is almost 100 times more alkaline than ammonia (pH 11.1).

A **lake** in a limestone environment neutralizes acid rain that falls in it. Its pH is maintained between 7 and 8, and animals and plants develop normally, since they are adapted to this pH level.

HOW ACID RAIN FORMS AND AFFECTS THE ENVIRONMENT

The widespread use of fossil fuels in motor vehicles and in industry causes the release of sulfur dioxide ❶ and nitrogen dioxide ❷ into the atmosphere. When these products combine with water ❸ from clouds, they form sulfuric acid ❹ and nitric acid ❺. The polluted clouds are carried by the wind ❻, sometimes thousands of miles (km) from the source of the pollution, before precipitation in the form of rain ❼ and snow ❽ returns the acids to Earth. These pollutants may directly reach watercourses ❾ or penetrate into the soil ❿, where they fix and transport certain chemical elements, including aluminum, lead, and mercury, to the water table ⓫.

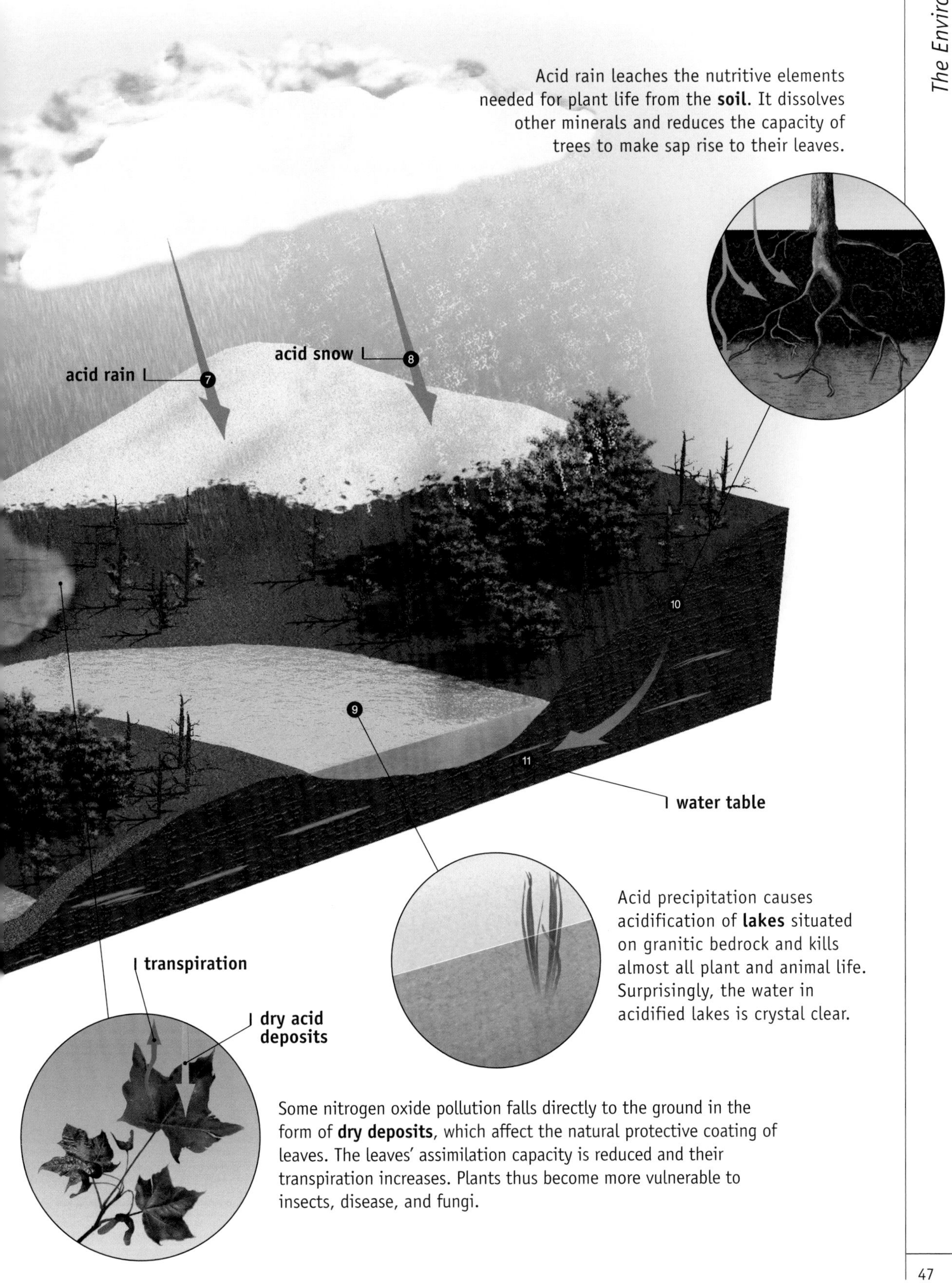

Acid rain leaches the nutritive elements needed for plant life from the **soil**. It dissolves other minerals and reduces the capacity of trees to make sap rise to their leaves.

acid snow ⌐———— 8

acid rain ⌐———— 7

10

⌐ **water table**

11

Acid precipitation causes acidification of **lakes** situated on granitic bedrock and kills almost all plant and animal life. Surprisingly, the water in acidified lakes is crystal clear.

⌐ **transpiration**

⌐ **dry acid deposits**

Some nitrogen oxide pollution falls directly to the ground in the form of **dry deposits**, which affect the natural protective coating of leaves. The leaves' assimilation capacity is reduced and their transpiration increases. Plants thus become more vulnerable to insects, disease, and fungi.

Sources of Water Pollution

The world's trash can

Many human activities, including industrial and agricultural processes, mining, urban street cleaning, and even household cleaning, eject wastewater into the natural environment. Since water is constantly circulating around the planet, it transports and redistributes the pollutants that it carries, including pesticides, bacteria, and heavy metals. DDT—a chemical formerly used widely as a pesticide— sprayed on a field passes into a watercourse, reaches the water table, and ends up in the ocean. By this time, it has contaminated a number of environments.

Waves and tides carry **urban trash** abandoned on the shore.

industrial waste

When they degrade, the hull coverings of **large ships** release metals, which are harmful to fauna.

Until 1970, **nuclear waste** was submerged in the ocean.

offshore drilling

maritime accidents

rinsing and emptying of tanks

sewers

The burying of **domestic waste** can cause contamination of the water table.

PETROLEUM IN THE SEA

It is estimated that more than 6.6 million tons (6 million tonnes) of petroleum—about .2 percent of world production— are poured into the oceans each year. Although dramatic, major oil spills represent only a small part of this spillage; accidental releases from oil refineries and offshore oil-drilling platforms are the main sources of oil pollution in the oceans. Another source of hydrocarbon pollution is the rinsing and emptying of tanks on the high seas by the 3,000 active oil tankers, which leaves permanent petroleum trails along the main maritime routes. Finally, deliberate or accidental releases of oil from automobiles, factories, and oil tanks on land are transported by watercourses or sewers to the sea.

THE SEA: A GIGANTIC DUMP

In spite of the London Convention, which since 1972 has forbidden the release of household trash into the sea, huge amounts of garbage, including plastic packaging, cans, and fishing nets, continue to float on the surface of the oceans. In addition, many cities do not always treat their wastewater before pouring it into the sea. These untreated wastewater discharges contain noxious organic matter that can promote infections and excessive algae development, as well as chemicals that are toxic to the environment, such as detergents and deicing salt.

Cooling water from nuclear power plants, which is much warmer than the water into which it is released, disturbs the ecosystem.

The stagnation of water held back by **dams** encourages the concentration of chemicals and the breeding of germs that can cause diseases.

Mines release pyrite, which transforms into sulfuric acid when mixed with oxygen and water. This toxic product gets distributed into the river network when retaining basins leak.

THE ORIGIN OF WATER POLLUTION

POLLUTION FROM THE LAND
- deliberate pollution (20%)
- accidental pollution (24%)

POLLUTION IN THE SEA
- accidental pollution (46%)
- deliberate pollution (10%)

Fertilizers, pesticides, insecticides, and herbicides used in **factory farming** infiltrate the water.

Use of **manure** in factory farming of cattle increases the quantity of nitrates in the soil and the water table.

Leakage from **septic tanks** may pollute water in the subsoil, as do pesticides used on domestic and public lawns.

Some old **underground reservoirs** that used to hold gasoline leak and release hydrocarbons into the water table.

Water Pollution

Effects on the environment and on humans

Because water is a vital resource for all living beings, water pollution is one of the most serious environmental problems. Not only can detritus, or waste from living organisms, injure aquatic animals, but the introduction of toxic elements—organic or inorganic—into the water seriously upsets ecosystems, fosters the development of epidemics, infects food chains, and causes the extinction of certain animal and plant species.

THE PHENOMENON OF DYSTROPHICATION

The natural enrichment of a lake with nutritive substances is called eutrophication. Without human pollution, this phenomenon takes place very slowly, through runoff water that drains organic materials. An excess of certain nutritive materials causes dystrophication of the aquatic environment and can have dramatic consequences.

Exxon Valdez,
1989

water supply   **solar light**

In a normally oxygenated basin, there is a variety of fauna, the water is clear, there are few algae, and sedimentation is limited.

COASTAL POLLUTION

	polluted coastal zones
	oil spills

Burmah Agate,
1979

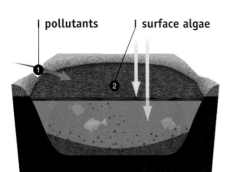

pollutants   **surface algae**

Different forms of pollution, such as industrial effluents, agricultural fertilizers, and sewer waste, can lead to an excess of phosphates or nitrates ❶ in the basin. Too much of these nutritive materials stimulates the growth of surface algae ❷.

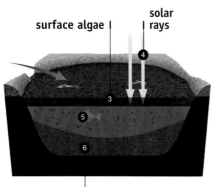

surface algae   **solar rays**

The thickening of the layer of surface algae ❸ blocks the Sun's rays ❹. Deprived of light, the lake-bottom algae die, which causes oxygen-consuming bacteria to multiply. Some of the aquatic fauna ❺ disappear for lack of oxygen, while the bottom of the basin fills with organic sediments ❻. At the end of the process, the water is totally deprived of oxygen and releases ammonia and hydrogen sulfide.

organic sediments

POTABLE WATER, DISEASES, AND COASTAL POLLUTION

Access to high-quality potable water varies widely around the world. Almost all populations in industrialized countries in the Northern Hemisphere have the benefit of clean water and of wastewater evacuation and treatment systems. Inhabitants of the poorest regions of the globe, on the other hand, are very often deprived of such services, and they are exposed to all sorts of diseases through their water.

Clean water is an essential component of public health. It is estimated that 25 million deaths each year can be attributed to infectious diseases, including cholera, typhoid, dysentery, and hepatitis, and parasitic diseases, such as malaria and schistosomiasis, transmitted by unclean water.

On the other hand, coastal pollution, due to industrial waste, agricultural products, and urban effluents, is localized mainly in the wealthy regions of the world, such as the North Sea and the Gulf of Mexico. The Mediterranean Sea is the site of both dystrophication and hydrocarbon pollution.

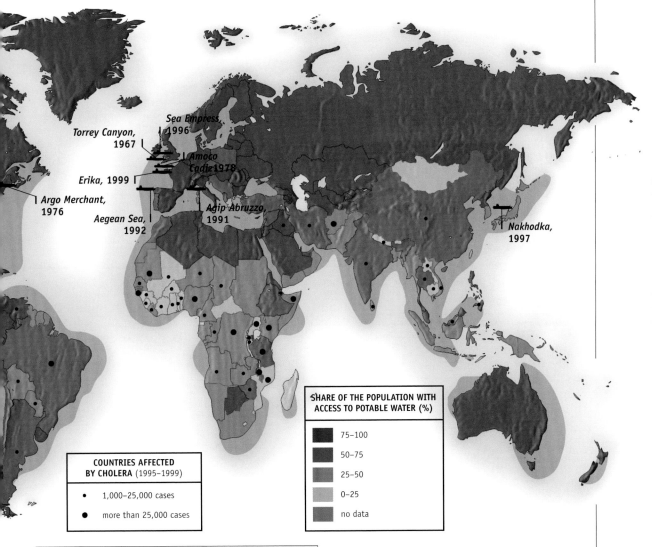

Sea Empress, 1996
Torrey Canyon, 1967
Amoco Cadiz 1978
Erika, 1999
Argo Merchant, 1976
Aegean Sea, 1992
Agip Abruzzo, 1991
Nakhodka, 1997

COUNTRIES AFFECTED BY CHOLERA (1995–1999)

- •   1,000–25,000 cases
- ●   more than 25,000 cases

SHARE OF THE POPULATION WITH ACCESS TO POTABLE WATER (%)

- 75–100
- 50–75
- 25–50
- 0–25
- no data

OIL SPILLS

Large oil spills that deposit sludge on the coasts are the most visible manifestation of ocean pollution. Although hydrocarbons are biodegradable, their decomposition can take years, and traces of oil remain for a very long time at the site of a spill.

Treatment of Wastewater

Purifying polluted water

Water used in various human activities becomes loaded with many organic and chemical residues. This wastewater, which often contains harmful materials, can have a disastrous effect on the environment if it is not properly treated before being released. It must undergo a complex purification process to keep it from polluting the natural environment.

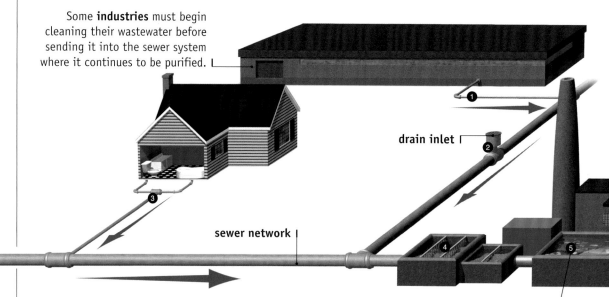

Some **industries** must begin cleaning their wastewater before sending it into the sewer system where it continues to be purified.

drain inlet

sewer network

desilting basin

PRIMARY MECHANICAL TREATMENT

Wastewater from industry ❶, streets ❷, and residences ❸ is collected in the sewer system. The first step in purification is removal of coarse solids through a process called screening ❹. The water is then sent to a desilting basin ❺, where minerals and dense particles settle to the bottom and are evacuated to a landfill site. This operation removes abrasive materials, which can damage pumping equipment. Oil removal, which is possible because of the difference in density between grease and oil as opposed to the water in which they float, is also carried out during this step. These floating materials are evacuated to a digester ❻.

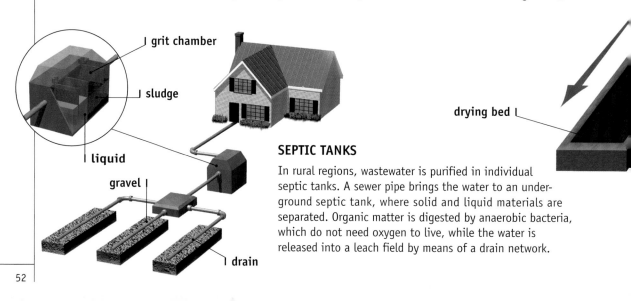

grit chamber

sludge

liquid

gravel

drying bed

SEPTIC TANKS

In rural regions, wastewater is purified in individual septic tanks. A sewer pipe brings the water to an underground septic tank, where solid and liquid materials are separated. Organic matter is digested by anaerobic bacteria, which do not need oxygen to live, while the water is released into a leach field by means of a drain network.

drain

DECANTATION AND BIOLOGICAL PURIFICATION OF WATER

Once it has been rid of its solid materials, wastewater is routed to a settling tank ❼, across which it flows slowly. Debris suspended in the water are deposited at the bottom of the basin in the form of sludge, which is raked and evacuated to a digester.

The settled water then passes into an aeration basin ❽ to undergo biological purification. Colonies of aerobic bacteria, constantly supplied with oxygen, feed on the organic pollution in the wastewater and agglomerate in a chemical sludge. The bacteria produce stable composites, including carbon dioxide, water, and minerals, and more sludge, which is kept suspended in the water by means of constant stirring.

The water is then pumped to a clarifier ❾, where it is separated from the remaining sludge by settling. Some of the recovered sludge is reintroduced ❿ into the aeration basin, where the microorganisms that it contains maintain the process. The rest of the solid residues are sent to the digester, while the water undergoes a series of additional treatments ⓫ before finally being released into the environment ⓬.

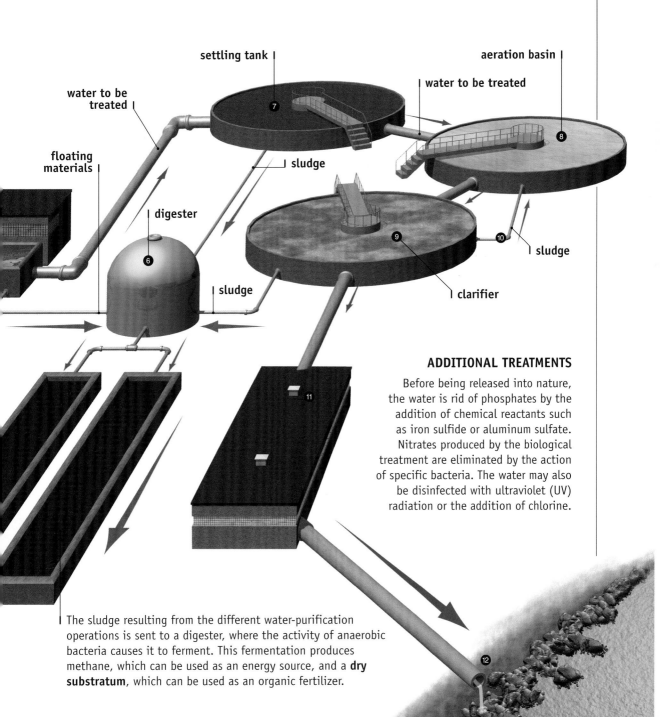

ADDITIONAL TREATMENTS

Before being released into nature, the water is rid of phosphates by the addition of chemical reactants such as iron sulfide or aluminum sulfate. Nitrates produced by the biological treatment are eliminated by the action of specific bacteria. The water may also be disinfected with ultraviolet (UV) radiation or the addition of chlorine.

The sludge resulting from the different water-purification operations is sent to a digester, where the activity of anaerobic bacteria causes it to ferment. This fermentation produces methane, which can be used as an energy source, and a **dry substratum**, which can be used as an organic fertilizer.

Soil Pollution

Each year, we release millions of tons of industrial waste, household trash, fertilizers, and pesticides into our natural environment. Organic materials, which contain carbon, are biodegradable—that is, they can be decomposed by microorganisms—and disappear relatively rapidly. But inorganic products, which are increasingly numerous and varied, infiltrate the ground, where they form toxic residues that poison the environment. In spite of government efforts to regulate waste elimination and agricultural practices, contamination of the soil remains a pressing concern.

When they are not recycled, discarded **automobiles** are a major source of soil pollution. Their batteries contain lead and acid, their oil infiltrates the water table, and the plastics and rubber tires they use decompose very slowly.

Tar can rise to the surface many years after being buried.

DOMESTIC POLLUTION

Household trash is composed mainly of organic materials, which can be degraded by bacteria in the soil. However, it also includes plastics, detergents, solvents, and heavy metals such as lead, mercury, and cadmium, that decompose more slowly, if ever.

A **landfill site** is an excavation into which domestic and industrial waste is dumped and covered by successive layers of dirt. Although landfill sites are sealed with a plastic film or a clay footing, runoff of rainwater causes some pollutants to infiltrate the subsoil.

SOIL SALINIZATION: AN UNEXPECTED FORM OF POLLUTION

In regions with a dry climate, the water table is usually very deep. Bushes, grasses, and other types of vegetation are dispersed ❶. The establishment of farms in dry climates requires the installation of irrigation systems ❷. The additional water from irrigation saturates the ground, which causes the water table to rise. The salts present in the water table rise with it toward the surface ❸. When the water table reaches the surface, the water evaporates, concentrating its salt in the upper layers of the soil. This salty crust poisons plants.

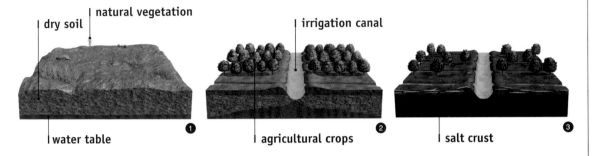

natural vegetation

dry soil

irrigation canal

water table

agricultural crops

salt crust

❶ ❷ ❸

mercury

lead

trichlorethylene

detergents

PCBs

INDUSTRIAL POLLUTION

Most nonbiodegradable pollutants in the soil come from industry, which releases more than 700 substances. Mercury, used in batteries and paints, causes serious sensory and motor problems in human beings. Lead, a heavy metal used in car batteries, is a toxin that causes symptoms including anemia, nausea, coma, and blindness. PCBs (polychlorinated biphenyls) release dioxin, a very toxic chlorinated product, as they degrade. Trichlorethylene is an industrial solvent that induces a coma when it is ingested.

tires

factory farming of livestock

spraying of fertilizer and pesticides

AGRICULTURAL POLLUTION

Intensive agriculture is a major source of pollution. Fertilizers increase the amount of nitrates and phosphates in the soil, upsetting the natural nitrogen and phosphorus cycles. Pesticides, herbicides, and fungicides sprayed over crops act indiscriminately on the entire ecosystem and disrupt the food chain at the same time.

As a result of intensive cattle and hog farming, large quantities of nitrates from animal dung are deposited into the soil and then infiltrate the water table.

water table

Desertification

How land becomes barren

Due to the combined effects of drought and human activity, more and more arable regions—like the Sahara Desert 2,000 years ago—are being transformed into deserts. Scientists estimate that between 12 and 15 million acres (5 to 6 million hectares) of Earth's arable land are affected by desertification every year.

THE ARAL SEA DRIES UP

The drying up of the Aral Sea—once the fourth-largest landlocked sea in the world in area—is a direct consequence of the huge project, begun in 1954, of irrigating the Karakum Desert, located on the border of Kazakhstan and Uzbekistan. When the Syr Darya and Amu Darya rivers were diverted to promote cotton production, the main water influxes of the Aral Sea were eliminated, and the sea was gradually reduced to two small lakes. By 2000, the Aral Sea was 60 percent smaller in area than it was in 1960, its volume had dropped by 80 percent, and, because the mineral salts from the water do not evaporate, its salinity had risen to 4.5 percent.

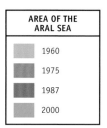

AREA OF THE ARAL SEA
1960
1975
1987
2000

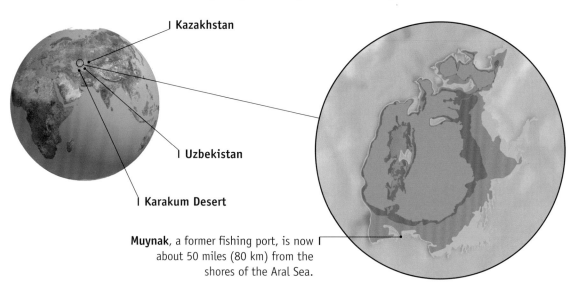

Kazakhstan

Uzbekistan

Karakum Desert

Muynak, a former fishing port, is now about 50 miles (80 km) from the shores of the Aral Sea.

AGRICULTURE AND DESERTIFICATION

Desertification sometimes results from abusive or improvised agricultural techniques. Overexploitation of land through monoculture, overgrazing, or deforestation destroys soils that a fallow season would have preserved.

Wild vegetation in **unexploited zones** protects semiarid regions from erosion and drought.

The **planting of crops** and deforestation of these wild zones makes the soil fragile.

Intensification of agriculture impoverishes the land, which is often then converted into pastures for livestock grazing.

THE STERILIZATION OF THE SAHEL

The Sahel, which extends from Senegal to Sudan, is one of the regions most affected by desertification. The sterilization of its soil is the result of a half century of intensive agriculture. In the past, the periodic monsoon rains ❶ ensured wild vegetation ❷ would grow in the region, protecting the land from the Sun's heat, returning moisture to the atmosphere, and, thus, contributing to the water cycle. In cultivated fields ❸, on the other hand, solar rays are absorbed directly by the soil, causing it to dry out.

The increase in farming in the region, due to a large number of new settlers in its towns, has exacerbated the drying of the soil. The disappearance of wild vegetation because of farming has resulted in dry, windy conditions ❹, creating windblown landscapes ❺ and causing the formation of sand dunes ❻.

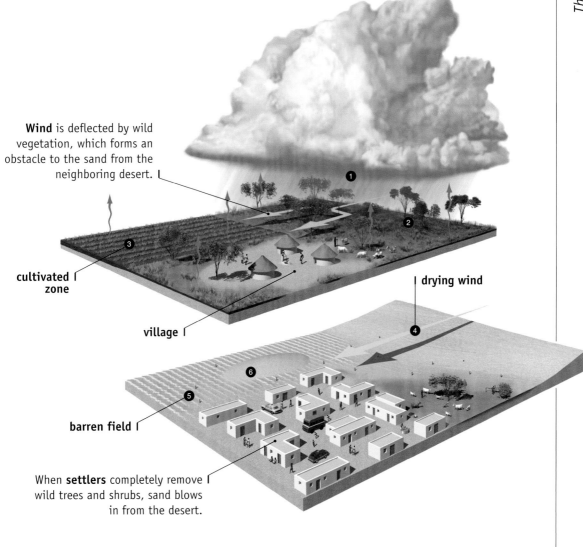

Wind is deflected by wild vegetation, which forms an obstacle to the sand from the neighboring desert.

cultivated zone

drying wind

village

barren field

When **settlers** completely remove wild trees and shrubs, sand blows in from the desert.

The land, now **sterile**, is abandoned by farmers.

By grazing on the last traces of vegetation, animals complete the **destruction of the soil**.

When it is totally dry and deprived of vegetation, the region enters the last stage of **desertification**.

Nuclear Waste

Pollution for the very long term

The nuclear power industry, which fulfills the energy needs of many countries, produces a wide variety of radioactive residues. Some of these, such as uranium and thorium, will take millennia to decompose into stable elements. Previously released directly into the oceans, these extremely toxic wastes are now stored in hermetically sealed and insulated containers. It is not known, however, if these precautions are sufficient to guarantee long-term safety.

EARTH'S CONTAMINATED SITES

In spite of precautions, a number of nuclear power plants have had major accidents. The site of the nuclear power plant in Chernobyl, Ukraine, is so contaminated that it will be uninhabitable for many years. Tests conducted by nuclear military powers such as the United States, the former Soviet Union, France, the United Kingdom, China, and India have also resulted in many sites being condemned, especially in the Pacific Ocean.

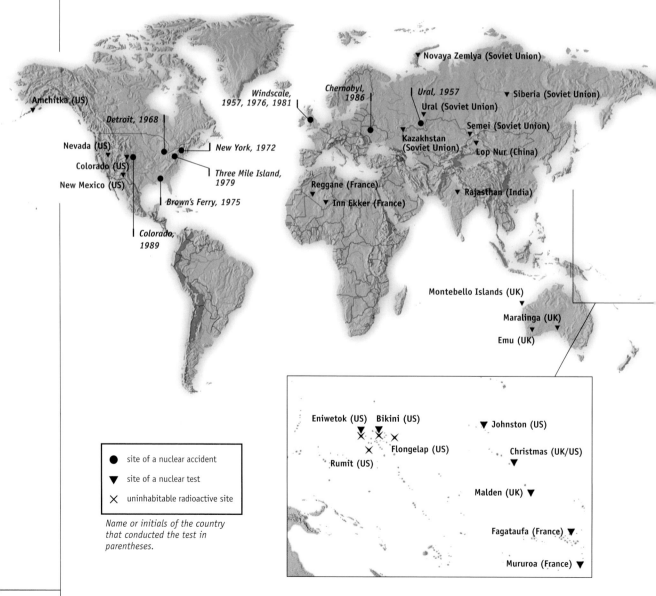

Novaya Zemlya (Soviet Union)

Amchitka (US)

Windscale, 1957, 1976, 1981

Chernobyl, 1986

Ural, 1957

Siberia (Soviet Union)

Ural (Soviet Union)

Detroit, 1968

Semei (Soviet Union)

Nevada (US)

New York, 1972

Kazakhstan (Soviet Union)

Lop Nur (China)

Colorado (US)

Three Mile Island, 1979

New Mexico (US)

Reggane (France)

Rajasthan (India)

Brown's Ferry, 1975

Inn Ekker (France)

Colorado, 1989

Montebello Islands (UK)

Maralinga (UK)

Emu (UK)

Eniwetok (US)   Bikini (US)

Johnston (US)

Flongelap (US)

Christmas (UK/US)

Rumit (US)

Malden (UK)

Fagataufa (France)

Mururoa (France)

- ● site of a nuclear accident
- ▼ site of a nuclear test
- ✕ uninhabitable radioactive site

Name or initials of the country that conducted the test in parentheses.

Pollution of the Food Chains

Effects of pollutants on living beings

Whether they are released into the water, the air, or the ground, pollutants disperse quickly into an ecosystem. Sooner or later, they enter a food chain and are transmitted from species to species, up to human beings.

THE POLLUTION CYCLE

Pollutants released by humans into the environment contaminate the water and ultimately enter human bodies by different paths, including the atmosphere we breathe, the plants and animals we eat, and the water we drink.

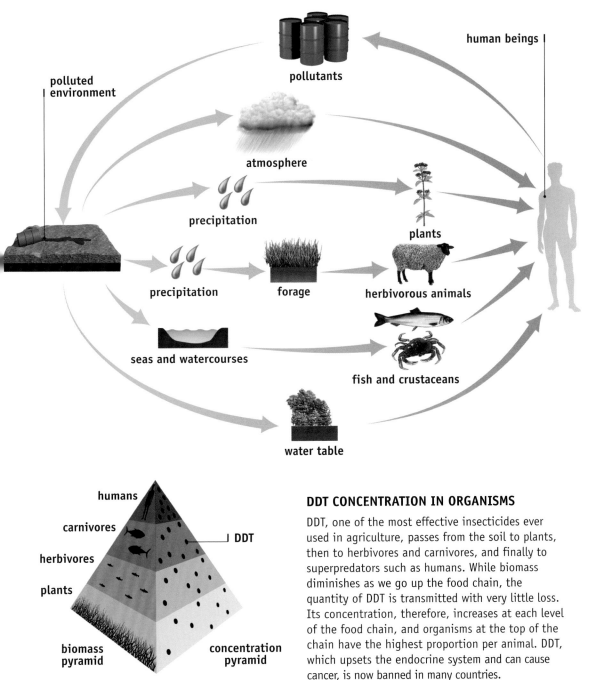

polluted environment

pollutants

human beings

atmosphere

precipitation

plants

precipitation

forage

herbivorous animals

seas and watercourses

fish and crustaceans

water table

humans
carnivores
herbivores
plants

DDT

biomass pyramid

concentration pyramid

DDT CONCENTRATION IN ORGANISMS

DDT, one of the most effective insecticides ever used in agriculture, passes from the soil to plants, then to herbivores and carnivores, and finally to superpredators such as humans. While biomass diminishes as we go up the food chain, the quantity of DDT is transmitted with very little loss. Its concentration, therefore, increases at each level of the food chain, and organisms at the top of the chain have the highest proportion per animal. DDT, which upsets the endocrine system and can cause cancer, is now banned in many countries.

Recycling

The Environment

Most waste can be recycled using a process specific to the material. Some materials—including extremely useful materials such as glass and aluminum—can be recycled and used many times over without noticeable changes occurring in the quality of the finished product. Because of this, recycling leads to major savings of raw materials and energy.

RECYCLING PAPER

Paper is soaked in water, stirred, and heated until it is transformed into pulp ❶. The pulp is screened ❷ and then placed in a centrifuge ❸, which extracts the ink and impurities such as staples. When the surplus moisture is drained off ❹ and the pulp is pressed ❺, it becomes paper once again ❻.

RECYCLING CARDBOARD

Cardboard is submerged in a soaking basin until it is transformed into pulp ❶. The pulp is then screened ❷ and placed directly into a press ❸, where it solidifies into new sheets of cardboard ❹.

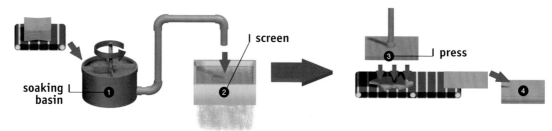

RECYCLING PLASTIC

The metallic impurities in flakes of plastic are eliminated using ferromagnetic processing (overband) or Foucault currents ❶. The plastic flakes undergo a final sorting in a flotation basin ❷, with the lightest materials remaining on the surface, and are then transformed into granules by an extruder ❸. The granules obtained are melted in a thermoforming furnace ❹ and molded into finished products.

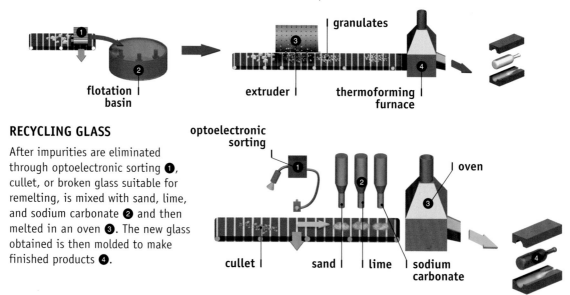

RECYCLING GLASS

After impurities are eliminated through optoelectronic sorting ❶, cullet, or broken glass suitable for remelting, is mixed with sand, lime, and sodium carbonate ❷ and then melted in an oven ❸. The new glass obtained is then molded to make finished products ❹.

RECYCLING METALS

Pieces of metal that can be recycled come in a wide variety of sizes and types, from cans, to scraps, to automobile bodies. They are first shredded in a pulverizer ❶. The particles obtained are sorted with a magnetic device ❷ and sometimes enriched with raw materials ❸. The metal, with or without additives, is melted in a blast furnace ❹ and then molded into ingots ❺. These ingots are transformed into sheets of metal ❻ that are used in the manufacturing of many types of products ❼.

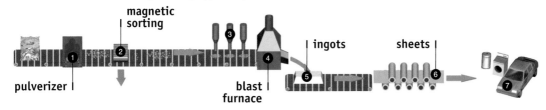

RECYCLING RUBBER

Old tires are shredded in a pulverizer ❶, which then also transforms them into powder. The powder goes through a magnetic sorting process ❷ that eliminates metallic impurities. Synthetic materials such as polyurethane ❸ are added to the powder, and the resulting mixture is then molded to produce flooring, soundproof panels, and solid tires ❹.

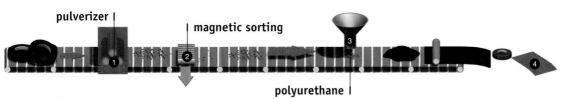

COMPOSTING

Taking several months, composting is a slow process for decomposing organic waste naturally. Materials are first sorted manually ❶ to ensure that they can be composted and are then ground up ❷ and sorted mechanically ❸. The ground organic material is then dried ❹ and enriched with ligneous materials ❺, such as wood chips and sawdust, to facilitate the decomposition process. When placed in a silo ❻, the mixture undergoes aerobic fermentation as a result of controlled temperature, humidity, acidity, and aeration. The final product of this process, called compost ❼, is used as a natural fertilizer.

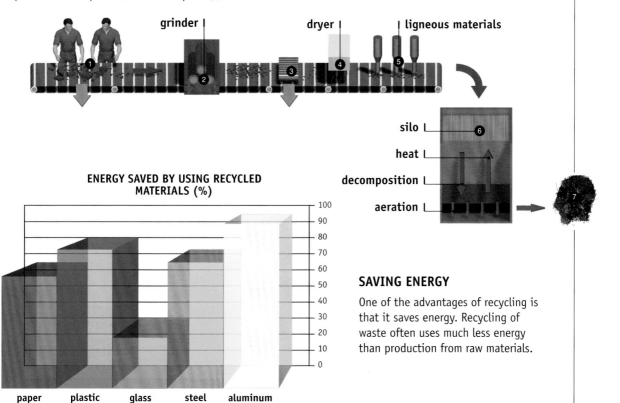

ENERGY SAVED BY USING RECYCLED MATERIALS (%)

SAVING ENERGY

One of the advantages of recycling is that it saves energy. Recycling of waste often uses much less energy than production from raw materials.

Glossary

anaerobic: Able to develop in the absence of air or free oxygen.

anticyclone: A zone having high atmospheric pressure.

atmospheric pressure: The pressure exerted by Earth's atmosphere.

biomass: The total mass of all living things in an environment.

chlorophyll: The green substance in most plants that enables photosynthesis.

convection: Ascending movement of a fluid caused by a difference in temperature.

Coriolis force: The deflection of a body in motion caused by Earth's rotation.

DDT: Dichlorodiphenyl-trichlorethane.

denitrification: Transformation of nitrates into molecular gaseous nitrogen through the action of specific microorganisms.

fallow: Plowed and left unseeded so that the soil will regain its fertility.

fertilizer: Any substance added to soil in order to promote growth of crops.

gelifraction: The process of fragmentation of rock beneath the ground caused by the force of the freezing of infiltrating water.

hydrocarbon: Any molecule, such as methane (CH_4),

benzene (C_6H_6), made only of carbon and hydrogen.

icecap: An area covered with thick, permanent ice, found especially in polar regions.

infrared: Having to do with electromagnetic radiation, the wavelength of which is between that of visible light and that of microwaves.

ions: Atoms or molecules that have lost or gained electrons and, thus, have a positive or negative electrical charge.

lichens: Composite plants formed from the association of a fungus and an alga, usually living attached to a trees or rocks.

ligneous: Woody or resembling wood.

littoral: Having to do with the shore of a lake, sea, or ocean.

microwave: An electromagnetic wave whose frequency is above 1 GHz.

mixed forest: A forest that contains both deciduous and coniferous trees.

monoculture: The use of land for growing only one type of crop.

monsoon: Related to the winds of Southeast Asia and the Indian Ocean that bring heavy, seasonal rains.

nitrate: A salt of nitric acid.

oasis: A fertile area in the middle of a desert resulting from the exposure of the underground water table.

orbit: The usually elliptical path of one celestial body around another.

parent rock: The deep, intact rock from which soil is formed.

pole: Each of the two points, the North Pole and South Pole, on Earth's surface through which the axis of Earth's rotation passes.

potable: Fit for drinking.

radioactive: Emitting energy generated by changes in the nuclei of atoms.

sludge: Semisolid residues resulting from water purification processes.

talus: A sloping mass of rocky fragments formed at the base of a cliff.

trade winds: The nearly constant, easterly prevailing winds that blow over the tropics and subtropics.

tropics: The terrestrial parallels located at 26°23′ latitude north (Tropic of Cancer) and south (Tropic of Capricorn), corresponding to the places at which the Sun is highest at the solstices.

tropopause: The boundary between the troposphere and the stratosphere.

ultraviolet: Having to do with invisible electromagnetic radiation, the wavelength of which is between that of light and that of X-rays.

water table: The area of underground soil and rock that is saturated with water.

Books

Basics of Environmental Science. Michael Allaby (Routledge)

The Climate Revealed. William J. Burroughs (Cambrige University Press)

Deserts (Ecosystem). Michael Allaby, Richard Garratt (Illustrator) (Facts on File, Inc.)

El Niño and La Niña: Weather in the Headlines. April Pulley Sayre (Twenty First Century Books)

Encyclopedia of Weather and Climate. Michael Allaby (Facts on File, Inc.)

The Facts on File Weather and Climate Handbook (The Facts on File Science Handbooks). Michael Allaby (Facts on File, Inc.)

Oceans (Ecosystem). Trevor Day (Facts on File, Inc.)

Ozone and Climate Change: A Beginner's Guide. Stephen J. Reid (Taylor and Francis)

Temperate Forests (Ecosystem). Michael Allaby (Facts on File, Inc.)

The Two-Mile Time Machine. Richard B. Alley (Princeton University Press)

Videos and CD-ROMs

Acid Rain (Earth at Risk). (Schlessinger Media)

Air Pollution, Smog, and Acid Rain. (Library Video)

Biomes Collection (five videos). (Library Video)

Chasing El Niño! (Nova)

Food Chains and Webs (CD-ROM). (Cyber Ed, Inc.)

The Ozone Layer (Earth at Risk). (Schlessinger Media)

Web Sites

El Niño: Online Meteorology Guide
ww2010.atmos.uiuc.edu/(GH)/guides/mtr/eln/home.rxml

Encyclopedia of the Atmospheric Environment
www.doc.mmu.ac.uk/aric/eae/index.html

Major Biomes
www.nhq.nrcs.usda.gov/WSR/mapindx/biomes.htm

Weather and Climate
members.aol.com/bowermanb/weather.html

Index